HOW TO MAKE PARTY AND HOLIDAY DECORATIONS

JANE BERRY

HOW TO MAKE PARTY AND HOLIDAY DECORATIONS

CHILTON BOOK COMPANY
Radnor, Pennsylvania

Jane Berry is also the author of *Christmas Creations*,
published by Chilton Book Company in 1974

Copyright © 1976 by Jane Berry
First Edition   All Rights Reserved
Published in Radnor, Pa. by Chilton Book Company
and simultaneously in Don Mills, Ontario, Canada,
by Thomas Nelson & Sons, Ltd.

Designed by Adrianne Onderdonk Dudden
Manufactured in the United States of America

Library of Congress Cataloging in Publication Data

Berry, Jane.
How to make party and holiday decorations.

(Chilton's creative crafts series)
1. Holiday decorations.   I. Title.
TT900.H6B43   1976   745.59'41   75-46508
ISBN 0-8019-6230-7
ISBN 0-8019-6231-5 pbk.

● *This book is dedicated to Doreen Snodgrass, a true friend,*
my daughter, Sue, and my Jack.
Without their many hours of help and endless encouragement
this book would not have been completed.

CONTENTS

ACKNOWLEDGMENTS

A book like this is not the work of one person. I had the help of many friends and associates. In addition to Doreen, Sue, and Jack, I thank Betty Johnson, Edna Libby, Gil Snodgrass, and Dolores Wright for their help. Thanks also to my editors Crissie Lossing and Lydia Driscoll for their help.

Credits for individual projects:

Ginny Mathews	*Fourth of July Driftwood Centerpiece*
Linda Snodgrass	*Swim Party*
Diane Snodgrass	*Xyla*
Dorothy English	*Jelly Bead Fantasy*
Ada Smith	*Be-Witched*
Joseph Sheridan	*Father's Day Centerpiece*
Ginny Bedford	*Fourth of July Picnic and Father's Birthday*

Materials used in the projects are courtesy of the following manufacturers:

Chenille	D. Jay Products, Inc.
	Newark, NJ
Glue	Bond Adhesives Company
	Jersey City, NJ
Ribbon and Lace	Lion Ribbon Company
	Bronx, NY
Styrofoam and Decorative Puff	Snow Foam Products, Inc.
	El Monte, CA
Decotiques and Wood Box	Heirloom Crafts
	York, PA
Decalon	Sangray Corporation
	Pueblo, CO
Quilling	Quill Art, Inc.
	St. Louis, MO
Wire Frames	Novelcraft Manufacturing Co., Inc.
	Rogue River, OR
Photographs	Gary Pugh
	Media, PA
	John T. Chew, Jr.
	Villanova, PA

LIST OF ILLUSTRATIONS

LIST OF COLOR
ILLUSTRATIONS

✦ 1 ✦

BEFORE YOU BEGIN

Crafts are fun and exciting. Crafts are a way of expressing yourself. Everyone has creative ability, so don't be afraid to try your hand at it. Once you learn the basics of working with the materials used in this book, try to do your own thing.

What a personal way to make gifts for someone you care about! If you make the gift, a little bit of you goes with it. The recipient will surely appreciate the thought, time, and effort that went into the gift.

Making your gifts and decorations is also economical. And when someone says how nice it is, you can proudly say, "I made it myself!"

You will need your own special craft clutter corner. An extra bedroom or a spot in the basement or the garage would be great.

For the projects in this book, a variety of materials have been used. You will find that you already have many of the items around your house and the others are readily available in craft and hobby shops, variety stores, hardware stores, and even the supermarket. Products such as Styrofoam, different types of chenille, liquid drape, Decorative Puffs, diamond dust, Decotiques, Liftables, Swistraw, and quilling paper can be found at craft and hobby shops. Make a visit to your local craft stores and take a look at the many new items and materials available.

Please don't hurry your projects. Always give paints and glues ample time to dry. You will be much happier with the outcome of your efforts.

Kits for some of the projects described in this book are available. Please send a self-addressed stamped envelope for information on kits to:

Jane Berry
301 Kirk Lane
Media, PA 19063

· Work Box ·

You should have a work box or reserved shelf to store the tools most frequently used in your craft work. For collectibles and remnants, a plastic shoe box is handy, so you can see into it to find what's on the bottom.

Some of my students use a sewing caddy found in department stores. It has many compartments for your supplies. Cover the outside with ribbon or pretty wrapping paper and spray with a protective glaze. You can then damp wipe any smudges away.

I suggest to my students that they wear old clothes or make a smock from an old robe, house dress, or man's shirt.

The supplies you need most often you should have in your work box. Here are a few:

pen or pencil	X-acto knife
notepad	straight pins
white glue, thick and thin	toothpicks
#28 spool wire	craft sticks
wire cutters	needle and thread
scissors	ruler
serrated-edge knife	paint brushes, ¼″ and ½″

There are other supplies I keep on a shelf in a handy spot in my workshop. They are:

spray adhesives	masking tape
#618 glue	Scotch tape
sparkle glitter	waxed paper
acrylic paints and stains	needle-nose pliers
jar for brushes	poster board
paper towels	felt scraps
floral adhesive	ribbon scraps
floral tape, assorted colors	chenille pieces

Before you begin, always read the directions very carefully on the label of the product you're using. There are many similar products on the market, but each will have its own method of application for best results.

Keep a card file for your own use. If you find short cuts or little hints while working with a certain material, be sure to make a note and file it.

· Flower Drying ·

If you plan to dry flowers or weeds, pick them in the morning. For drying fresh flowers from your garden, I suggest using silica gel. They will keep most of their true color. Most craft shops and florists carry this product.

Some weeds such as cattails, dock, or goldenrod, can be dried by tying the stems together and hanging upside down in a dry area, such as a closet or garage.

· Chenille ·

The word *chenille* comes from the French language and describes a hairy caterpillar. The chenille used in craft work today is made of rayon, nylon, and acetate fibers protruding from a wire case. There are many types and sizes of chenille. And the colors are radiant.

Regular chenille stems are the most popular. Some people call them pipe cleaners. They are 12 inches long and about ¼ inch in diameter. There are also jumbo chenille stems. They are about ½ inch in diameter. The stems have many uses, such as making flowers, flower stems, wrapping items together, or hangers for mats.

Chenille also comes in bump form. The 3-inch bump is the most popular: it comes 10 bumps to the yard. The 1-inch bump comes 28 bumps to the yard; the 2-inch, 18 bumps to the yard. Recently, larger bumps have become available. The 5-inch bump comes 7 to the yard and 7-inch comes 5 to the yard.

Loopy chenille comes by the yard. It's great for making poodles, bows, and flowers.

Curly chenille is just what it says. It reminds me of little girls' long curls. It's terrific as hair for dolls or figurines. You can become a hairdresser using the curly chenille.

Chenille is a very versatile craft product. Because it comes in so many sizes and colors, there is no end to project ideas. It can be cut with scissors or wire cutters. I feel chenille is one of the great craft materials on the market today. The possibilities range from simple little ideas to very artistic displays.

· Ribbons ·

Working with ribbon is really a pleasure. It comes in many colors, patterns, sizes, and finishes. You have ginghams, polka dots, plaids, florals, stripes, and plain. Some of the finishes are cotton, acetate, burlap, velvet, and satin. The colors are so bright and alive.

Ribbons can be cut to any width to fit your project. Many ribbons are fray proof, but cut a small piece and test it for raveling. If it does ravel, put a thin line of glue on the line you wish to cut, let it dry thoroughly, then cut.

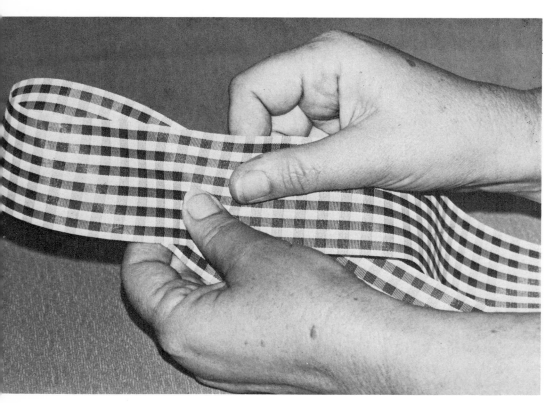

Fig. 1-1 *Forming the first loop for a bow.*

Fig. 1-2 *The second and subsequent loops are formed the same way.*

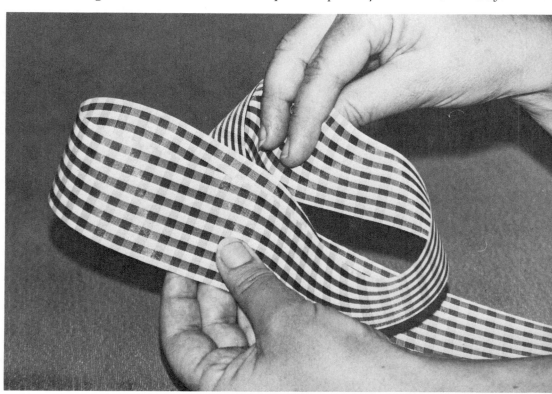

Sizes and ribbon numbers are as follows:

Number	Width
#1½	$5/16''$
#2	$7/16''$
#3	$5/8''$
#5	$7/8''$
#9	$1^7/16''$
#16	$2''$
#40	$2¾''$
#100	$4''$

The materials lists for the projects give both the number and width of ribbons required. In some projects you will trim the ribbon to size when a project calls for a special width.

· MAKING A BOW ·

Figures 1-1 through 1-3 show the basic steps in making a bow. The width of the ribbon and the number of loops depends, of course, upon the project, but the basic procedure is the same. Make the first loop, leaving an appropriate amount on the end loose for a streamer. Make

Fig. 1-3 Using a length of chenille stem to fasten the bow at the center of the loops.

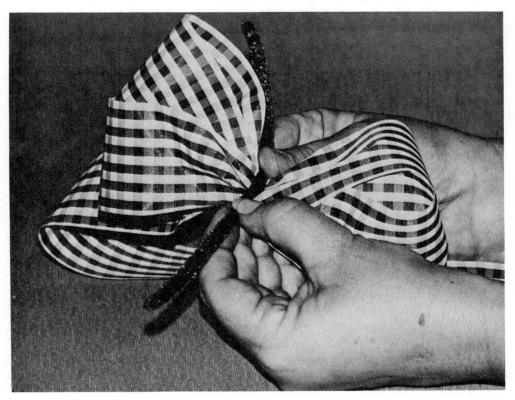

another loop on the other side, leading the ribbon to the back. Catch the ribbon at the center after each loop.

Repeat the steps to make as many loops as you want, then fold a length of wire or chenille stem over the center of the bow. Twist the wire around the ribbon, leaving the ends free to attach the bow to your project. Glue a length of matching ribbon over the wire to hide it. Once you've mastered the technique of making a bow, you'll want to put one on every project you make.

· Glues ·

Bond Gr-r-rip and Solio are nontoxic liquid white cements. They are free flowing, so I suggest using these for applying prints to plaques, felt to cardboard, etc. They will not penetrate fabrics, dry clear, and form a powerful bond. Easy cleaning, too—they peel off your fingers and the brush can be washed out in water.

Bond's 484-Tacky and Slomon's Velverette are heavy glues, hold instantly, and do not soak through fabrics. There is nothing I dislike more than working on a vertical craft project and having the glue run and drip on everything. If you do need glue somewhat thinner, just add a little water. These glues can be used on most all craft materials. They dry clear and are nontoxic. I think they are great!

Bond #618 is what I use for gluing Styrofoam to Styrofoam, and trimming Styrofoam. It dries very, very fast and clear.

Also, Bond spray adhesive and spray mirror clear glaze are used throughout the book.

· Styrofoam ·

Styrofoam is an essential material for craft work. It's a great medium to build on and from. It can be painted, cut, shaped, and glued. You may use it as is or cover it with chenille, ribbon, felt, etc. Houses, people, cars, and flowers can be made from Styrofoam. The possibilities are numerous. You'll think of new ideas constantly as you work with it.

To cut Styrofoam, use a serrated-edge knife or a heated cutting knife. To shape Styrofoam, such as flattening a ball, just roll on the table top to compress. Finer shaping can be done by pushing and pressing with your fingers.

When buying spray paint, finishes, or glazes, be sure that they can be used on Styrofoam if this is your intention. Some sprays will dissolve Styrofoam. Remember to always read the labels.

· Protective Finishes ·

There are many protective finishes available today, both in spray and brush applications. These materials can be found in craft shops, paint and hardware stores. Read the label on the product you are buying to be sure it is compatible with the materials you are using in your project.

Clear acrylic sprays are the quickest and easiest to use. They come in gloss and matte finishes. Use the gloss glaze for a shiny surface and matte for a dull coating. Spray varnish also gives a durable, smooth finish.

Polymer medium and brush-on acrylic finishes are suitable also as protective coatings on your finished projects. Be sure that the surfaces are clean before brushing on any finish. Use a clean brush for application and allow each coat to dry thoroughly before applying another coat.

· New Materials ·

Tinsel tex wire is a metallic cord wrapped around wire; it resists tarnish. It is good for making flowers and various trim accents and is used for several projects in this book.

Decorative Puff is a fluffy glass filament that comes in batt form. It comes in sheets of various sizes and can be cut with a razor blade or scissors. It can also be pulled apart to make different thicknesses. I suggest that you always cover your hands and arms with talcum powder before starting to work with Decorative Puff.

2

NEW YEAR'S EVE

· Gala Invitation ·

For a hard-to-refuse invitation, you can't beat this handmade one, shown in color in Figure 1.

MATERIALS

4″ x 9″ piece black construction
   paper
18″ silver braid
1 package iridescent sequins

2″ x 2″ hot pink felt
2″ x 2″ green felt
scissors
white glue

INSTRUCTIONS

Fold the construction paper in half to a 4-inch by 4½-inch size. Run a thin line of glue around the four edges. Press the braid into the glue. Turn the corners with the braid, do not cut it.

Form the numeral outline of the new year with sequins along the bottom 4½-inch side, then glue the sequins in place. Glue two sequins in each top corner.

Following the pattern outline in Figure 2-1, cut one hat each from pink felt and green felt. Next cut a narrow piece of each color of felt for a hatband. Be sure to cut them long enough. Cut a small piece of felt of each color in the shape of a feather.

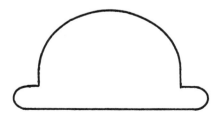

Fig. 2-1 Hat pattern for New Year's party invitation.

Glue the green hatband and feather on the pink hat, and the pink hatband and feather on the green hat. Glue the hats in position on the construction paper and trim each hat with sequins.

· *Father Time* ·

No welcome to the new year is complete without a visit from old Father Time (color section, Fig. 1). He'll be the life of your party.

MATERIALS

24″ x 36″ white sheeting or thin cotton material
liquid draping solution
9″ or 10″ plastic detergent bottle
3″-diameter Styrofoam ball
1¼″-diameter Styrofoam ball
18″ of #16 wire
1 cup sand or pebbles
aluminum foil
masking tape
pink spray paint

4″ x 11″ white fake fur
two 7mm wiggle eyes
4mm pink bead
6″ x 10″ brown felt
4″ x 8″ poster board
½ yd gold braid
10 straight pins
scissors
white glue
clear acrylic spray or hair spray
waxed paper

INSTRUCTIONS

Work on waxed paper on a table. Then, when you need to turn the project, turn the paper around. Do not lift the project!

Put a cup of sand or pebbles into the detergent bottle to give it weight. Cut a hole in each side of the bottle near the top and push the wire through the holes. Shape each end of the wire for the shoulders and arms, making a bend at both elbows. Tape wire to bottle at each shoulder so it will stay in place. Wrap the wire down to each wrist with aluminum foil. This prevents rusting of the wire.

Cut a piece of sheeting 24 inches by 24 inches. Fold the sheeting in half and then in half again so you now have a 12-inch square. Cut a ½-inch arch at the point where the folds meet. Open halfway and cut 8 inches from each side along the fold of the material. Cut two 5 inch by 7 inch pieces of sheeting for sleeves.

Pour draping solution into a plastic container and dip the sleeves into the solution as shown in Figure 2-2. Squeeze out the excess, but do *not* wring, as this causes wrinkles (Fig. 2-3). Fold under one 5-inch edge of each sleeve ¼ inch and press with fingers. This hems the raw edges of the cuffs. Lay one end of a sleeve over shoulder on bottle. Drape down over the covered wire, leaving ½ inch of wire free. Press the underarm seam together. Drape the other sleeve in the same manner.

Dip the large piece of sheeting into the draping solution. Squeeze out the excess and unfold. Place the center over the top of the bottle and bring the slits together under the arms, pressing the edges together. Gently drape and fold the sheeting around the bottle to resemble a robe. Fold a hem under at the bottom. Tie the gold braid around the waist. Let dry overnight.

Cut the 1¼-inch Styrofoam ball in half. Then, holding the pieces together, cut a small pie-shaped wedge out of the straight edge to form hands. Spray paint these two pieces and the entire 3-inch ball pink. When dry, place glue on the ends of the arm wires and push Styrofoam hands into place.

Push the 3-inch ball down over the bottle neck. Glue wiggle eyes and the pink bead nose into place. Cut a piece of fake fur 1½ inches by 3½ inches. Glue and pin into place for whiskers. Cut another piece of fake fur, 2½ inches by 7 inches. Lay it across the head and decide where you want the hairline. Then glue and pin into place. Comb some fake fur down over the forehead, then spray with clear acrylic spray or hair spray to keep the hair in place.

Fig. 2-2 Dipping fabric into liquid draping solution.

Cut the scythe from poster board, following the pattern in Figure 2-4. Spread glue on one side of the poster board and press onto the brown felt. Trim the felt following the poster board outline. Spread glue on the other side and repeat. Lay the scythe across Father Time's arm: you're now ready to decorate your table for New Year's Eve.

Fig. 2-3 *Squeezing liquid drape solution out of fabric.*

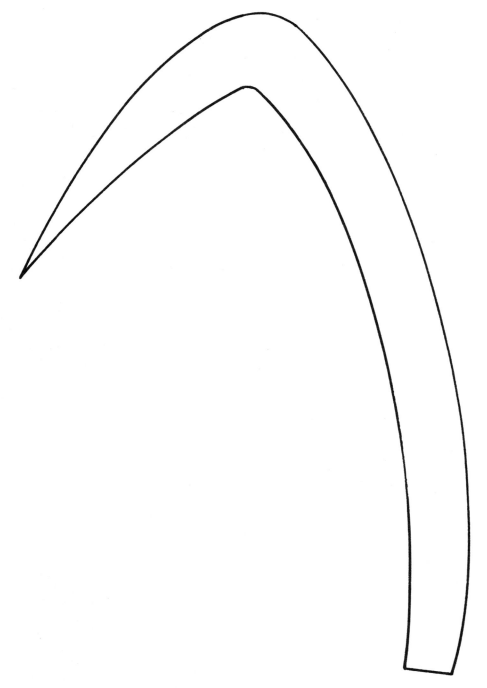

Fig. 2-4 *Pattern for the scythe carried by Father Time.*

· *Clock* ·

What better way to chime in the new year than with a clock especially made for the occasion? You can see the finished project in Figure 1, color section.

MATERIALS

3″-diameter Styrofoam ball
7″-diameter Styrofoam disc, 1¼″ thick
9″ x 18″ green felt
1⅔ yd single-loop gold braid
1⅓ yd of 1⁷/₁₆″-wide (#9) pink and white gingham ribbon
10 pink rondels
4 pink tri-beads

nine 8mm pink crackle beads
five 8mm pearl corsage pins
5mm pearl corsage pin
fourteen 3mm pearls
4 gold spangles
gold tinsel stem
pink chenille stem
scissors
white glue

INSTRUCTIONS

Spread glue over one side of the Styrofoam disc and lay it on one end of the green felt. Smooth out any wrinkles and press into glue. Trim off felt around the edge of disc. Repeat this step for the other side.

Cut the ribbon to fit the edge of the disc and glue around the edge. Glue gold braid around the disc right over the felt edge, both front and back. Set aside for a few minutes to dry.

Cut the 3-inch Styrofoam ball into quarters. You'll only use one piece. Cover all three surfaces with green felt. Be sure to stretch the felt as you work on the rounded side. Trim away the excess at edge. Then glue the gold loop braid around all the edges. This is the bell for the clock.

Divide one flat side of the disc into quarters and mark. This will be the clock's face. Glue a gold spangle at each mark to represent 12, 3, 6, and 9 o'clock. Over the hole in each spangle, first glue a pink tri-bead, then a 3mm pearl.

Cut two pieces of gold tinsel stem: one 2¼-inch length and one 2¾-inch length. Glue one end of each onto the center of the clock face—with the hands indicating 11:55. Make an arrow for each hand by gluing on five pink rondel beads, with a 3mm pearl in the center of each. Put an 8mm pink crackle bead on the 5mm pearl-headed corsage pin and stick into the center of the face at point where tinsel stems meet.

Put two 8mm pink crackle beads on each of four corsage pins. Push these into the bottom of the clock for legs. Once you have them balanced, glue into place.

Spread glue on one *flat* side of the felt-covered bell. Attach to the top of the clock where the long hand points. Hold for a few minutes until the glue dries. Cut a 5-inch piece of pink chenille stem. Twist it around the remaining corsage pin, making the twist ½ inch long. Then push the pin into the top of the bell.

· *Champagne Favors* ·

For New Year's Eve favors, try making the small champagne glasses shown in the color section, Figure 1. You can make them in many colors, add fake fur for hair and beads for earrings. Try to make them resemble friends that you've invited: for a golfer, a small golf club; for an avid musician, a tiny horn; for a teacher, a small book.

MATERIALS

for two favors:

2″-diameter Styrofoam ball
1¼″-diameter Styrofoam ball
white chenille stem
½″ x ½″ each of pink, white, blue, and red felt

½″ x 1½″ green felt
5″ of ⁵/₁₆″-wide (#1½) pink ribbon
tiny flower
pink bead
2″ length of #28 wire

INSTRUCTIONS

Cut the two balls in half. Cut two 2-inch pieces of chenille stem. Join one half of the 2-inch ball to one half of the 1¼-inch ball, using a piece of chenille stem. Assemble the two halves so that the rounded sides face each other and the chenille is the glass stem. The large piece is the top of the glass, and the smaller piece is the base.

For eyes, cut four ¼-inch-diameter circles, two from pink felt and two from blue felt. Cut four white circles, ⅛ inch in diameter. Glue tiny white circles onto the blue and pink circles. Then glue in place on the glasses for eyes—pink for the lady, blue for the man. Cut two ¼-inch red circles for mouths. For the lady's mouth, cut out a pie-shaped wedge. Then glue each mouth in place.

Make a tiny bow with pink ribbon. Secure the bow with wire, glue the flower in the center, then glue the bow at the base of the lady's glass. For the man, cut a small tie from green felt and glue onto stem of his glass. Glue a pink bead in position for knot of the tie.

These can be used as place cards—let your guests try to find themselves!

3

VALENTINE'S DAY

· *Valentine Place Card* ·

This delightful, individualized place card is shown in Figure 3-3.

MATERIALS

2″ x 6″ red Decorative Puff
5″ x 5″ piece white construction
 paper
2 tiny white flowers
18″ red tinsel cord

red chenille stem
red felt-tip pen
scissors
white glue

INSTRUCTIONS

Following the pattern in Figure 3-1, cut out a heart from white construction paper. Glue red cord around the edge of the heart and set aside to dry.

Gather the Decorative Puff in the center and secure gathers with a 3-inch piece of chenille stem. Twist stem at the back and cut away the excess. Now glue into position on the heart. Glue two tiny white flowers in the center of the heart.

Write a guest's name on the heart to use as a place card or a gift card.

· *Heart's Delight* ·

Figure 3-2 shows another idea that could be used for many occasions by changing the color and trim. How about using green Decorative Puff flowers and tiny pipes for St. Patrick's? Or black flowers and orange chenille pumpkins for Halloween?

Fig. 3-1 Heart pattern for individual place cards.

MATERIALS

24″ of 2″-wide (#16) red acetate
   ribbon
Styrofoam block, 4″ wide, 8″ long,
   2″ thick
package of red Decorative Puff
seven #18 stem wires
red floral tape

21 tiny white flowers
42″ of 2″-wide (#16) red
   gingham ribbon
7 white chenille stems
white glue
scissors
pliers

INSTRUCTIONS

Glue the red acetate ribbon around the edges of the Styrofoam block
and set aside to dry. On one end of each stem wire, bend over 2 inches
into a hook shape. Do not close the hooks.

    The sheet of Decorative Puff I used was 12 by 24 inches. Pull it
apart so you have only one-half the thickness with which to work. Cut
seven strips, each 4 by 12 inches. Gather one strip at the center and
slide the wire hook over the center to secure the gathers. Using pliers,

Fig. 3-2 Doug's Valentine (wall hanging), Heart's Delight, place card, and Valentine Sundae.

twist the end of the hook around the stem. Repeat until you have seven flowers, then wrap each stem with red floral tape.

If you've never used floral tape before, here's how it's done. Hold the stem in your left hand and the end of the tape in your right. Let the roll lay on the table. Roll the wire between your left thumb and index finger. Guide the tape with right thumb and index finger and wrap tightly as you whirl the wire around. Wrap the tape at a slant and overlap it—it will stick only to itself. When you reach the end of the wire, tear the tape. Assemble all your flowers.

Glue three tiny white flowers in the center of each red flower.

Take two flowers and lay one wire against another with one flower just below the other. Tape the two wires together. Lay the third flower below the first two and cut the wire so the completed stem is 15 inches long. Push this stem into the Styrofoam block 3 inches from the left end and an inch from the back. All stems will go into the Styrofoam at this spot.

Now with the flowers facing you, carefully bend the top one to your right, giving it a gentle curve. Bend the next one to the left, the third to the right.

Cut the stem on the fourth flower to measure 6 inches long. Push it into the Styrofoam so that the flower extends above the left corner of the Styrofoam block. The wire for the fifth flower should be 5 inches long and for the sixth flower, 7 inches long. Push these into the Styrofoam so the fifth flower is above the center of the block and the sixth flower is above the right corner.

Make a four-loop bow from gingham ribbon (*See* Ch. 1, Making a Bow). Secure by twisting a 3-inch piece of chenille stem at the center of bow. Cut a point into the ribbon ends. Push the bow into the Styrofoam to cover the bases of the flower stems. Cut the wire on the seventh flower to measure 2½ inches long and push it into the Styrofoam above the center of the bow. Bend the flower to cover the center of the bow.

To make a heart, first measure 7 inches on a chenille stem, but do not cut it. Bring the end of the 7-inch length around to form a loop and twist the cut end around the stem. Hold the twist in your right hand. With your left thumbnail, make an indentation about ¼ inch deep and presto!—you have a heart shape. Make six more hearts the same way.

One heart should go at the top of your centerpiece. Twist the end around the flower stem to secure it in position. Put another heart 5 inches directly below the top one. Place one heart above the bow, one at the right side of the Styrofoam block, and three at the back extending above the flowers.

· *Doug's Valentine* ·

One evening, a group of friends were conferring in our workshop when Doug Libby suggested the idea for the festive wall hanging shown in Figure 3-2.

MATERIALS

12″ Styrofoam heart	3″-high Styrofoam cone
red glitter	floral adhesive
spray adhesive	2 craft sticks
24″ circular rattan mat	24″ wooden dowel, ¼″ diameter
3 yd of 2″-wide (#16) red gingham ribbon	white acrylic paint
	paint brush
3 yd of 1⁷⁄₁₆″-wide (#9) red acetate ribbon	newspaper
	box lid
red chenille stem	white glue
3″ x 3″ Styrofoam block	

Lay newspapers on the floor and place the Styrofoam heart on them. Spray with adhesive. Pick heart up carefully. Hold the heart over a box lid and sprinkle with red glitter. Shake off any excess glitter into box lid. Set the heart aside to dry for 30 minutes. Pour the leftover glitter from the lid back into the container.

Cut the Styrofoam cone in half from tip to base and cut the dowel in half. Put glue on one end of one dowel and push it into the half cone. Paint both pieces of dowel white. When the heart and dowel are dry, push one piece of dowel into each side of the heart for an arrow. Line up both pieces of the arrow and then glue into place. Let dry completely.

Run the gingham ribbon through the open weave of the mat. Then run the red ribbon around the outside of the gingham. Cut off any extra ribbon and glue the ends together on the back of the mat.

Put floral adhesive, the size of a fifty-cent piece, on the back of the 3-inch Styrofoam block. Press the block into the center of the mat. Push one half of each craft stick into each corner of the block. Center the heart over the block and carefully press the heart onto the craft sticks.

Lay the red ribbon along the center of the gingham ribbon. While holding the two together, make a four-loop bow (*See* Ch. 1, Making a Bow). Secure at the center with a 6-inch piece of chenille stem. Twist the stem at the back. Push the remainder of the stem through the bottom center of the mat and twist at the back, securing the bow in position.

· *Valentine Sundae* ·

For a sweetheart or a sweet tooth, the super sundae shown in Figure 3-3 fills the bill nicely.

MATERIALS

6″ Styrofoam ball	scissors
10 yd of 3″ white bump chenille	5½ yd silver tinsel tex wire
14 red chenille stems	6″-diameter plastic container
pencil	(Cool Whip)

INSTRUCTIONS

Cut the Styrofoam ball in half—you'll only use one piece for this project. Be sure the diameter of plastic container and half ball are the same. Push the flat surface of the half ball into the container. Make sure it's a tight fit.

Cut all the white bump chenille into single bumps. For the first row, just above the edge of the container, push one end of a chenille

Fig. 3-3 Place card and Valentine Sundae.

bump into Styrofoam. Pull chenille bump 1½ inches to the right and push the other end of chenille bump into Styrofoam. Push one end of the second bump into the Styrofoam at the center of the first bump; the other end 1½ inches to the right. Continue around the half ball so that there are 18 scallops in the first row.

For the second row, push one end of chenille bump into Styrofoam ½ inch above first row. Push the other end into the Styrofoam ⅛ inch to the right of the first end. Now twist the bump halfway to the right and press the loop against the Styrofoam toward the first row. Continue this process until there are 20 bumps in the second row.

Fig. 3-4 Double-heart bow pattern for Valentine Sundae.

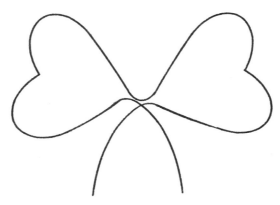

The rest of the Styrofoam is covered in the same manner as the second row. Use 18 bumps in row three; 16 bumps in row four; 12 bumps in row five; 8 bumps in row six; and 4 bumps in row seven, the last row.

Using a 12-inch red chenille stem, shape a double-heart bow following the pattern in Figure 3-4; make four bows altogether. Cut four pieces of red chenille stem, 2 inches long each, and bend into V shapes. Put the V over the point where the double hearts meet and push the ends of the V into Styrofoam at edge of container through the center of a scallop. Put another heart bow directly opposite. Put two more heart bows at points along the edge, dividing the sundae into quarters.

Cut nine red chenille stems, each 10 inches long, and shape each one into a heart. Put a heart between the bows. Place another heart an inch directly above each bow. Heart number nine goes at top center.

Cut thirteen pieces of tinsel tex wire, each 12 inches long. Twist each wire around a pencil to make a coil, leaving ½ inch straight at one end. Push the coils into the Styrofoam at center of each heart and each bow.

Enjoy your Valentine Sundae.

4

ST. PATRICK'S DAY

· *Shamrock Favor* ·

Time for the wearin' o' the green is upon us; the first step in getting ready for the celebration is the party favor shown in color, Figure 2. This is another idea that can be varied for almost any holiday or party. Change the colors and trim to suit the occasion.

MATERIALS

3″ x 3″ white felt
1 kelly green jumbo chenille stem
12″ kelly green braid
14″ of $^5/_{16}$″-wide (#1½) kelly green velvette ribbon
7″ of 1$^7/_{16}$″-wide (#9) kelly green and white gingham ribbon

plastic or metal container or spray can top, 1½″ high and 2″ in diameter
scissors
white glue

Fig. 4-1 Pattern for Shamrock Favor.

Glue the gingham ribbon around the container. Cut a 6-inch piece of chenille stem and shape it into an arch for the handle. Glue the handle in place and hold for a few minutes until the glue sets up. Then glue the velvette ribbon around top and bottom edges of the container, covering the ends of the handle.

Use the pattern in Figure 4-1 to cut the shamrock from white felt. With a thin line of glue, secure braid around the edge of the shamrock. Glue the shamrock to the center of the handle. Fill the favor cup with green and white mints and it's party time!

· Leprechauns ·

Wouldn't a dozen of these cute little guys, shown in Figure 2, color section, be great sitting across the center of your buffet table!

MATERIALS

for two figures:
3 kelly green jumbo chenille stems
two 1¼"-diameter Styrofoam balls
8" x 8" kelly green felt
3" x 3" white felt

4" x 5" black felt
½" x ½" red felt
four 7mm wiggle eyes
scissors
pencil
white glue

INSTRUCTIONS

First let's cut the hats from the kelly felt (Fig. 4-2). Roll each one into a cone shape, overlapping the edges ⅛ inch, and glue together. Cut two pieces of black felt, each ¼ inch wide and 5 inches long. Cut buckles from white felt (Fig. 4-2). Glue the black bands around bottom of hats, ¼ inch from the edge. Keeping in mind the seam is in the back, glue a white buckle in center front of each hat.

Cut eight hands from the white felt, four feet and four leggings and shoes from the black felt, following the patterns in Figure 4-2.

Now from the jumbo chenille stems, cut four pieces 4 inches long for legs and two pieces 5 inches long for arms.

Push two leg pieces side by side into the Styrofoam balls. Lay one 5-inch arm piece across the top of the legs snugly against the ball, and twist the ends across each other, bringing the arms to opposite sides. Trim ¼ inch of the chenille off the stems at ends: this makes it much easier to glue on the felt hands and feet. Repeat for the other leprechaun.

For the hands, glue the two pieces together with the end of the stem between them. Remember to keep thumbs up.

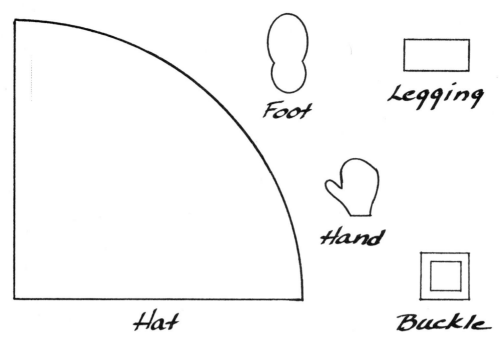

Foot

Legging

Hand

Hat

Buckle

Fig. 4-2 Hand, hat, foot, legging,
and buckle pattern for Leprechauns.

Glue the rectangular black leggings around stem ends of legs, then glue the shoe shape to the bottom of the legging.

Spread a thin line of glue on inside edge of a hat and put atop one ball, tilting it a little to one side. On one of the elves, fold the top of the hat down toward his shoulder and glue into place.

Cut small triangles of kelly felt for noses and quarter-moon shapes from red felt for mouths. Glue these and the wiggle eyes into position.

Arrange the arms and legs as desired and set one in your centerpiece and the other one on the hat wall hanging that you'll make in the next two projects.

· St. Patrick's Garden ·

MATERIALS

five 24″ kelly green chenille stems
3 jumbo kelly green chenille stems
4 jumbo white chenille stems
9″ of 2¾″-wide (#40) kelly green ribbon
18″ of 2¾″-wide (#40) green and white polka-dot ribbon
18″ of 2¾″-wide (#40) green and white gingham ribbon

6″ x 6″ kelly green felt
3″ Styrofoam ball
4″-square vase on pedestal
scissors
pencil
white glue
floral adhesive
6″ of #16 stem wire
6″ green floral tape

Slice a small piece from the Styrofoam ball to make a flat bottom. Now spread glue over rounded part of ball and cover with kelly felt. The felt will stretch, so pull and smooth out any wrinkles or folds. Put floral adhesive on uncovered flat area and press the ball into container.

Now it's time to make your shamrocks from the 24-inch chenille stems. Follow the pattern in Figure 4-3. Measure off 6 inches and bring short end of stem to the 6-inch mark, with ¼ inch overlap to twist around the stem. Put thumbnail at center top of loop and bend into a shamrock petal shape. With next 6 inches, form second loop and give a full twist at base to join to stem. Again shape with nail. Repeat for third petal, then bring stem up and over the center.

Spread glue on the back of the two *side* petals and press down onto

Fig. 4-3 Shamrock flower pattern for garden centerpiece.

Start Here

the ribbon. Let dry. Then trim carefully around edge of stem. Glue third petal onto ribbon and cut out when dry.

Make two shamrocks from gingham, two from polka dot, and one from solid kelly ribbons.

To form a coil, twist the seven jumbo stems, both green and white ones, around pencil, leaving 2 inches straight at the end of each stem.

Use your scissor point to make two ½-inch slits, crossing each other, in top center of felt-covered ball. This is where you'll push all stem ends.

With floral tape, secure stem wire to chenille stem of solid green shamrock. Push this into the Styrofoam. The top of shamrock should be 8 inches above container. Now put the polka-dot shamrocks on each side of the solid green shamrock, as shown in Figure 2, color section. Then secure the gingham shamrocks near the container. Shape the stems slightly so they fall over edge of container. Put the curled jumbo stems in as fillers.

· *Wall Hanging* ·

This hat wall hanging, shown in Figure 2 in the color section, is a perfect perch for leprechauns or other small folk.

MATERIALS

6″ half-round Styrofoam bell shape	2″ x 2″ white felt
9″-diameter Styrofoam ring	1½″ x 10″ black felt
emerald spray paint	white glue
14″ x 18″ black oval place mat	needle and white thread
2⅔ yd of 2¾″-wide (#40) green and whilte polka-dot ribbon	scissors
	6 toothpicks
1½ yd of 5/16″-wide (#1½) kelly green velvet ribbon	10 snap clothespins

INSTRUCTIONS

Cut the Styrofoam ring in half. Stick toothpicks halfway into flat side of ring, spacing evenly. Spread glue on the bottom of the half-round bell and press down over the toothpicks, making inside edges meet. The ring is now the hat brim.

Place the hat on newspapers and spray it with emerald paint. Let it dry for half an hour before handling.

While waiting, you can run a gathering thread down the center of the polka-dot ribbon and pull it up to half its original length. Measure carefully to make certain it goes around the edge of the place mat, then knot the end of your thread so the ruffles won't slip. Spread glue on the place mat about ¼ inch in from the edge and lay the ruffled ribbon on

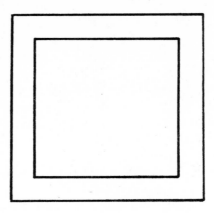

*Fig. 4-4 Buckle pattern for the hat in
St. Patrick's Day wall hanging.*

the glue. Slip snap clothespins over ruffle and mat to hold them together until the glue dries.

Glue the black felt around the hat for the band. Cut the buckle
from white felt, using the pattern in Figure 4-4. Glue it onto the center
front of the hatband.

When the ruffle is dry, remove the clothespins. Put a thin line of
glue down the center of the ruffle. Press the narrow velvet ribbon over
the gathering thread. I used velvet ribbon here, rather than another
kind, because the velvet is soft and easy to secure around the curved
edges.

Put a lot of glue on the back flat surface of the hat and press it into
the center of the place mat. Your pretty creation is ready to hang on
the front door—or over your buffet table—to greet your friends.

5

EASTER

· Bunny Favor ·

Figure 3 in the color section shows this cute little party favor—a delightful finishing touch for the table.

MATERIALS

two 1″-diameter Styrofoam balls
blue chenille stem
pink chenille stem
2″ x 5″ blue felt
6″ of 1⁷⁄₁₆″-wide (#9) pink
  polka-dot ribbon

6″ of #28 wire
two 5mm wiggle eyes
white glue
nut cup or soufflé cup
scissors
toothpick

INSTRUCTIONS

Attach one ball to the other with a toothpick and glue. Using the patterns in Figure 5-1, cut four ears, two feet and one bow tie from the felt.

Glue two ear pieces together with a ½-inch wire sandwiched in between for body. Leave ¼ inch of wire outside the ear at one end. Repeat for the other ear. Put glue on the end of the ear wires and push into appropriate spots on one Styrofoam ball.

Glue the eyes into place. Push the pink chenille stem into the head for a nose, then cut off flush with the ball. This is much easier than cutting a small piece of stem and trying to push it in place.

Now glue the bow tie at the neck and the feet on the bottom ball.

Cut two 1-inch pieces of blue stem and push into the Styrofoam for arms. Bend the arms at the elbows to give them shape.

Cut a 1½-inch piece of pink stem. Loop one end to make a tiny walking cane and glue onto one hand. Give the bunny a tail, using the same technique as you used to make the nose. Glue a scrap of pink polka-dot ribbon inside each bunny ear.

Cover the nut cup by gluing on sections of ribbon 1¼ inches wide at top and ¾ inch wide at the bottom. Fill the nut cup with jelly beans and stand the bunny in front. The children will love this favor.

Bow Tie

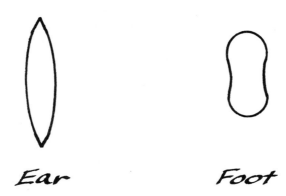

Ear   *Foot*

Fig. 5-1 Ear, foot, and bow tie pattern for Bunny Favor.

· *Easter Rabbit House* ·

You simply can't invite the Easter rabbit without a place for him to be warm and cozy! The perfect spot? A bunny house, of course—the completed project is shown in color, Figure 3.

MATERIALS

60 yd of 3″ copen blue bump chenille
54 yd of 3″ yellow bump chenille
45 yd of 3″ pink bump chenille
1 yd of 3″ emerald bump chenille
two Styrofoam sheets, 12″ x 36″ and 1″ thick

8 gold chenille stems
ruler, paper, and pencil
round toothpicks
3 grocery bags
white glue
scissors

INSTRUCTIONS

Enlarge the pattern pieces in Figure 5-2 onto paper, following the measurements shown. When everything is accurately drawn, cut out the parts to use as your pattern. Or simply transfer the dimensions directly onto the Styrofoam. Cut the house parts from the Styrofoam sheets, following the pattern.

Cut all the chenille into single bumps and separate by color, put-

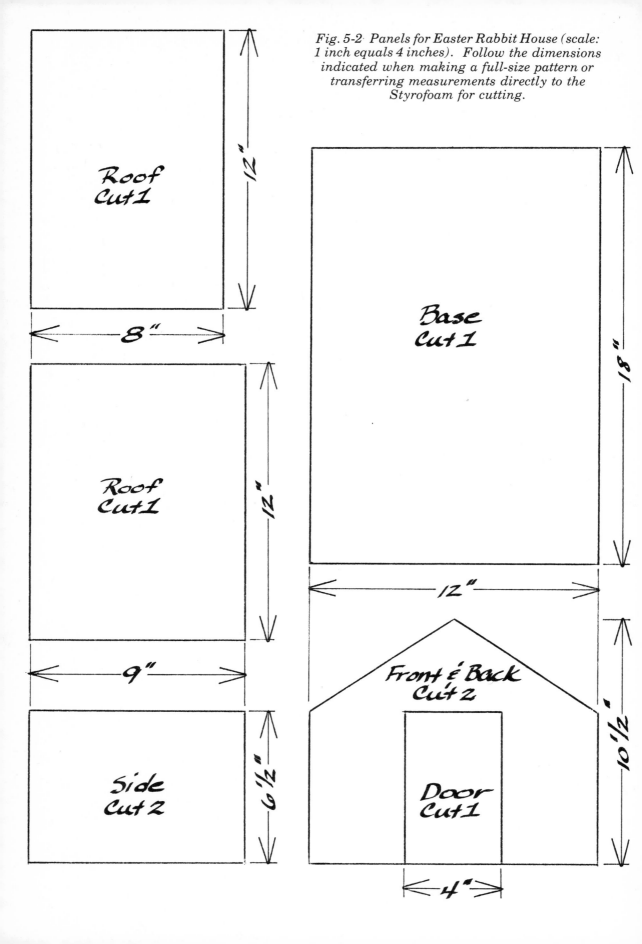

Fig. 5-2 Panels for Easter Rabbit House (scale: 1 inch equals 4 inches). Follow the dimensions indicated when making a full-size pattern or transferring measurements directly to the Styrofoam for cutting.

ting all bumps of one color in a grocery bag. This is a great project to keep your hands busy while watching TV.

Let's work on the base first. Start in one corner and go the length of the Styrofoam. Push one end of a single pink bump into the Styrofoam and lay it flat toward the other end of the base. Push the second end into the Styrofoam. Make a row along the length of the Styrofoam, making sure that the ends of the bumps meet. For row two, start the second bump *over* the edge, so that the fat part of the bump will be where the chenille ends met in the first row. Complete row two in this manner. Continue to cover the entire base in this manner, alternating the starting point in each row.

To trim the edges of the base, push both ends of each bump into Styrofoam at the bottom. Twist each bump halfway and push in toward the top surface of the base.

To cover the walls of the house, attach the yellow bumps to the Styrofoam as you did the pink to the base. The bumps should run vertically on the Styrofoam, that is, run them up and down for the walls, rather than from back to front. Be sure to cover the inside edges of the doorway, but do not cover the edges of the four walls.

Insert three toothpicks halfway into the edges of each side wall, then glue along the edges. Push the other half of these toothpicks into the front house panel and the opposite ends into the back panel. Press firmly so that there is no gap. Finish covering the corners with yellow bumps.

Now, we'll work on the blue roof. Starting in the lower lefthand corner of either roof section, push both ends of one blue chenille bump into the Styrofoam at the edge and ¾ inch up from the bottom. Twist the bump halfway and press flat against the roof. Repeat this process to make a row across the roof; your rows will be ¾ inch apart. Cover both roof sections this way. You will have eleven or twelve rows. Do not cover the edges.

Put four toothpicks into the top edges of the front and back panels of the house, then glue these edges. Press the roof down onto the tooth-picks, one piece at a time. Be sure the roof hangs over the house pieces evenly. The roof should meet in an even peak.

Put two rows of bumps along all edges of the roof. Put two more rows of blue bumps over the peak seam.

Push toothpicks into the bottom edges of the house and spread glue here, also. Press the entire house into the base so that three sides are equal distances from the edges of the base, with a generous front yard.

The flowers in the front yard are made by cutting chenille stems at random lengths and making a coil on one end. Push the other end into the Styrofoam base. Then put two green bumps at the back of each flower arrangement.

· Bunnies ·

You can make these bunnies shown in Figure 3, color section, in any color. They would make a nice gift or favor for a party—and, naturally, you need someone to live in your Easter Rabbit House.

MATERIALS

for two bunnies:

forty 3″ copen blue chenille bumps
forty 3″ white chenille bumps
3 miniature straw hats
four 2″-diameter Styrofoam balls
four 10mm wiggle eyes
black chenille stems
2 white chenille stems

1″ x 1″ pink felt
1″ x 1″ black felt
tiny flowers
plastic eggs
white glue
round toothpicks

INSTRUCTIONS

Cut 35 white single bumps. Push one end of each bump into a Styrofoam ball and wrap halfway around the ball. Now push the other end into the ball. Repeat for second bump directly opposite the first bump, thus dividing the surface in half. It's much easier to cover the ball uniformly if you divide it this way. Now fill in the entire ball.

Cover the second ball in the same manner. Push two toothpicks into either ball at the point where chenille ends meet. Put glue on the other ball at same spot. Push the two balls together to form the head and body of your bunny.

Use 5 single bumps for arms, legs, and tail. Form each one into a loop and push ends into Styrofoam at the proper place. The arms are where the two balls join, the legs on the bottom of the same ball, and the tail at center back.

From the white chenille stems, cut two 3-inch pieces, one 2½-inch piece, and one 1-inch piece. Shape the one-inch piece into a U. Position the other three pieces on the face for whiskers. Push the ends of the U shape over the center of these whiskers into the ball to secure the position. Glue a small, pink felt circle into position for a nose. Cut out a black felt bow tie and glue at neckline. Glue eyes into place. Glue a straw hat on his head. Push a double-bump chenille section into the Styrofoam on each side of hat for his ears. Cut the black stem in half, shape as a cane and glue in his left hand.

Construct the girl bunny the same way, using blue chenille, omitting the cane, and adding flowers to her hat.

I used the other lacy hat as a nest, gluing plastic eggs in it.

Place your bunnies on the roof of *their* house or at the door of *your* house.

· Egg Tree ·

MATERIALS

Styrofoam cone, 5″ diameter at
   base, 12″ high
8 yd yellow loopy chenille
9 purple chenille stems

14 miniature plastic eggs
white glue
straight pins
scissors

INSTRUCTIONS

Spread glue on the bottom one-third of the cone. Make a hole with the
point of your scissors near the bottom edge of the cone. Put glue on the
cut end of the loopy chenille and push into this hole.

    Holding the cone at the top, where there is no glue, wrap the
chenille around the cone so that each row touches the other. Pin when
needed as you wrap. When you have covered the glued area, spread
more glue on the cone and cover that area. Continue until the cone is
completely covered. Secure the top end as you did the other at the
beginning.

    Cut seven purple stems in half. Shape each half into a bow. Secure
each bow in place by putting a 1-inch piece of chenille stem, shaped in a
V, over the center of the bow and pushing the ends into the Styrofoam.
You will arrange the bows in four rows at even intervals around the
cone. Put four bows in the first and second rows, three in the third row,
two in the fourth row, and one at the top. Glue a tiny egg at the center
of each bow.

· Jelly Bead Fantasy ·

*A friend made the Jelly Bead Tree Fantasy shown in color, Figure 3,
and is sharing it with us here.*

MATERIALS

two 1″-diameter Styrofoam balls
24″ of 2″-wide (#16) pink
   polka-dot ribbon
Styrofoam disc, 7″in diameter and
   1″ thick
9 chenille stems, assorted colors
2 blue jumbo chenille stems

2 pink jumbo chenille stems
1 white jumbo chenille stem
17 Jelly Beads
four 7mm wiggle eyes
12″ of #22 wire
scissors
white glue

INSTRUCTIONS

Trim the polka-dot ribbon to fit around the outside edge of the
Styrofoam disc and glue into place. Set aside to dry.

Cut six chenille stems into various lengths, none shorter than 7 inches. Leave three stems uncut. Glue a Jelly Bead to one end of each stem and curve that end. Put glue on the untrimmed ends of all stems and push them into the center of the disc.

To make one of the bunnies, cut four 4-inch pieces of blue jumbo chenille stem and a 5-inch piece of white. Trim some chenille off the end of each stem.

Glue a pair of eyes onto one Styrofoam ball. Shape two pieces of blue as ears and push into the top of the ball. Push two more blue pieces into the neck for legs and body. Wrap the white stem around the blue leg stems for arms, twisting the ends to opposite sides to secure them. Glue Jelly Beads to the arms for hands and to the legs for feet. Shape the legs in a sitting position and shape the arms, bending them at the elbows. Cut short pieces of wire, add glue, and insert in ball for whiskers.

Make another bunny the same way, using pink jumbo chenille where blue was mentioned. Glue the bunnies in place on the Jelly Bead Tree base.

Make a bow from the remaining ribbon and secure with a piece of chenille stem at the center. Attach the bow to the disc by pushing in the stem and glue a Jelly Bead in the center of the bow.

⚜ 6 ⚜

MAY DAY

· *Maypole Dance* ·

Dancing girls around the maypole make such a cute centerpiece. The ribbons available today are so colorful that creating a project like the one shown in color, Figure 4, is great fun.

· *DOLLS* ·

MATERIALS

for six dolls:

4″ each of blue, green, lavender, orange, pink, and yellow ribbon, 2¾″ wide (#40)
4″ x 4″ white net
12″ lace trim
14″ black curly chenille
14″ brown curly chenille
14″ yellow curly chenille
9 antique gold 1″ chenille bumps

3 lavender 1″ chenille bumps
6 white 1″ chenille bumps
3 white chenille stems
six 20mm wooden head beads
8″ x 9″ lightweight poster board
craft stick
scissors
white glue
pencil

INSTRUCTIONS

Cut one gown pattern (Fig. 6-1) from the poster board. Using the craft stick, spread glue over one side of the pattern and lay onto the *wrong* side of the lavender ribbon. Remember to fit the pattern at one end of the ribbon so as not to waste any ribbon. Smooth out any wrinkles carefully and lay aside for 10 minutes to dry. Then trim the ribbon around the edge of the pattern.

Choose one small and one large piece of ribbon from the remaining lavender scraps. On the wrong side of the ribbon, make a thin line of glue in the outline of one large (1-inch diameter) and one small (½-inch diameter) flower. Let these dry for 30 minutes and then use sharp scissors to cut out the flowers.

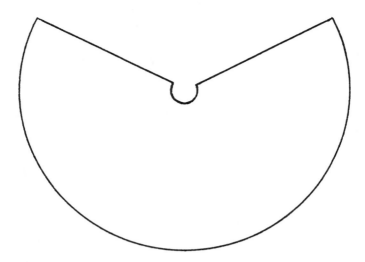

Fig. 6-1 Gown pattern for the May Queen and her attendants.

Pick up the lavender dress. Roll gently into a cone shape. Overlap the straight edges ⅛ inch and glue together. Hold the seam between your finger and thumb for a minute until the glue has a chance to set.

Cut a 5-inch piece of white chenille stem and fold in half. Put a dab of glue on one end of the stem and push into the hole in the wooden bead head, just *to* the opposite edge of the bead. Make sure the face is right side up. For hair, cut one piece of curly chenille 2½ inches long and glue around her little round face. Then glue a 4½-inch piece around and around, covering the rest of her head. You may choose to do different hairstyles, so have a try at being a hair designer and do your own thing. Once the hair is arranged, you must let it dry for 10 minutes—or it will slip around when you touch it.

It's time to attach her head to her body. Put a small amount of glue at the neck hole in the top of the dress. Push the chenille stem on which the head is mounted into the hole, leaving ¼ inch of stem for her neck.

Use the three 1-inch lavender chenille bumps for her arms. Lay the center bump at front of her neck. Wrap the chenille around to the back, cross over, and extend to the sides. Shape the chenille to resemble arms.

Find the two flowers you cut from matching ribbon: glue the small flower in the doll's left hand; glue the large flower at the center front of her head for a hat.

Follow these steps for the other five May Day girls, mixing the antique gold and white chenille bumps for arms with the gown colors in the arrangement you like best.

For my May Queen, I chose the blue ribbon. After gluing the poster board pattern to the wrong side of the ribbon, glue the right side of the ribbon to the white net. Allow to dry and cut out as for the others. Now glue lace trim around the bottom of the skirt. After you have assembled the Queen, glue a lacy crown on her head.

· MAYPOLE ·

MATERIALS

1⅓ yd of ⅜"-wide (#1½) yellow satin ribbon

28" of ⅜"-wide (#1½) lavender satin ribbon

28" of ⅜"-wide (#1½) green satin ribbon

38" of 2"-wide (#9) yellow burlap ribbon

12" yellow plastic tubing

2 bunches of cloth forget-me-nots

Styrofoam disc, 12" in diameter and 1¼" thick

12" x 12" square of grass cloth

13" wooden dowel, ¼" diameter

5"- diameter wooden hoop

white glue

INSTRUCTIONS

Glue the grass cloth to one surface of the Styrofoam base. Trim away the excess. Then glue the yellow burlap ribbon around the edge allowing about ¼ inch to extend above the top grassy surface.

Pull the cotton thread from inside the tubing. Slip the dowel inside the tubing, glue tubing to dowel at both ends, and let dry. Make a slit in the center of the disc for the maypole. Push the uncovered 1-inch end of dowel through the slit and into Styrofoam. Glue in place and let glue set.

Cut a 28-inch length of yellow ribbon. Glue the middle of all three 28-inch lengths of ribbon onto the top of the maypole. Make sure they are spaced *evenly* around the pole.

Now glue the remaining yellow ribbon around the outside of the wooden hoop. Have a friend help you now. Slip the hoop over the maypole and hold it about 5 inches from the top. Fasten it in place by tying each ribbon in a loose knot around the hoop. Space the ribbon knots evenly around the hoop, allowing the ribbons to drape to the base.

Assemble the May Queen and her attendants around the maypole, placing each one under a ribbon. Tie a ribbon loosely to each girl's right hand. Glue forget-me-nots atop the maypole, at its base, around the hoop, and around the base.

Your Queen and her court are now ready to perform their Maypole Dance.

· *Miniature May Basket* ·

This basket idea can be adapted to the theme of almost any party you might imagine. It is quick and easy to make, and joyously colorful, as you can see in Figure 4, color section.

Styrofoam disc, 2½″ in diameter, 1″ thick

14″ of 2¾″-wide (#40) yellow floral ribbon

4 orange chenille stems

twenty-four 8mm yellow crackle beads

18″ of 7/16″-wide (#2) orange burlap ribbon

craft stick

white glue

scissors

pencil

INSTRUCTIONS

Lay the Styrofoam disc on the wrong side of the yellow floral ribbon, near one end, and trace around the edge with a pencil. Do this twice, then cut the two circles. Use the craft stick to spread glue over one flat side of the Styrofoam disc. Lay the wrong side of one of the ribbon circles onto the glue and smooth out the wrinkles. Repeat, gluing the second circle on the other side.

Cut a piece of yellow floral ribbon 1 inch wide by 9 inches long. Spread glue on the edge of the disc and place this piece of ribbon around the Styrofoam disc. Cut the burlap ribbon into 9-inch sections and glue at the top and bottom of the edge. Set aside to dry.

We'll use one orange chenille stem for the handle. Slide eight yellow crackle beads onto the chenille stem, spacing them as follows: first bead 2½ inches from one end; then seven beads, each 1 inch apart; the eighth bead should be approximately 2½ inches from the other end of the stem.

Cut eight 4-inch lengths of chenille stem. Slide two crackle beads onto each piece, spacing them 1¼ inches from each end. Repeat, completing the seven remaining pieces. Dip the ends of the bead-trimmed chenille stem pieces into glue. Push one end into the Styrofoam at the outside edge next to the ribbon. Now bend the other end over in an arch and push into the edge of the Styrofoam approximately ¾ inch away. Position a second stem piece directly across from the first: this divides your area evenly and makes it easier to space all eight pieces of stem. Now divide into quarters and put in two more pieces. Then fill in the other four spaces.

You've already made the handle, so you're ready to affix it now. Center the handle and attach it at the outside edge just as you did the scallops.

Cut a piece of floral ribbon ½ inch wide and 8 inches long. Make a small bow and secure it at the center with a 2-inch piece of chenille stem, twisting one time at the back. Attach bow to the center of the handle by twisting stem around the handle.

· *May Basket Favor* ·

This variation of the May basket (color section, Figure 4) is used for favors. Make them in all the spring colors you used for the girls in the Maypole centerpiece.

Styrofoam disc, 2½″ in diameter
  and 1″ thick
28″ of 2¾″-wide (#40) lavender
  print ribbon
22″ of ⁵⁄₁₆″-wide (#1½) lavender
  ribbon

4-ounce paper cup
3 lavender chenille stems
eight 8mm purple crackle beads
3 purple dog bone beads
scissors
white glue

INSTRUCTIONS

Glue the print ribbon to the top and bottom surfaces and around the edge of the Styrofoam disc. Allow to dry and trim off excess.

Cut paper cup so it's 2 inches high, then glue ribbon to the sides: you will have to slit the ribbon in a few places so it will lay flat. Glue narrow ribbon to one edge of Styrofoam disc: this will be the top. Now glue narrow ribbon to the top of the cup, both inside and outside.

Cut one chenille stem 11 inches long for the handle. Slide one dog bone bead to center of the stem. Now slide one 8mm bead to each side of dog bone bead, an inch apart. Put a second 8mm bead on each side, an inch apart. Shape the stem into a U for handle. With the point of your scissors, make a small hole in top of Styrofoam disc at the edge. Put a dab of glue on end of stem and push into the hole. Repeat for the other end, directly across the disc.

Cut two chenille stems into 5-inch pieces. On each of two pieces slide dog bone beads to the center. Using the same method as you did to secure the handle, put one of these in the center of each side, with the ends of each stem one inch apart.

Glue the ribbon-covered cup onto the center of the disc.

Fold the other four 5-inch pieces of chenille in half. On each piece slide one 8mm bead to the center point. Form a U shape in each and glue one to each side of previous scallops.

Fill with candy treats or flowers.

· Gift Basket ·

If someone cannot attend the May Day celebration, decorate a basket and fill it with flowers and cookies for them.

MATERIALS

eight 10mm beads in assorted
  colors
eight 24″ chenille stems in
  assorted colors
2 yd of 2¾″-wide (#40) green and
  white gingham ribbon

green paint
wooden mushroom basket
paint brush
gesso
white glue
scissors

Brush two coats of Gesso over the entire basket, allowing it to dry for 30 minutes between coats. Then apply two coats of green paint. Let dry.

Glue the ribbon around the top of the basket, folding it over the top edge and gluing half to the inside and half to the outside of the basket. This gives it a more finished look. Cut the remaining ribbon in half *lengthwise* and glue one strip around the bottom of the basket. Wrap the handle with the remaining ribbon, gluing the ends down.

The flowers are formed from the 24-inch chenille stems by making seven loops to complete a circle. Slip a bead over the end of the stem at the center of the flower, then secure the petals by wrapping the remainder of the stem over the center of the flower and twisting it. Glue the flowers on the basket, three on each side and one on each end.

MOTHER'S DAY

· *Door Decor* ·

To greet your visitors on Mother's Day, create the friendly welcome for your door shown in Figure 7-1.

MATERIALS

18″ circular rattan mat
Styrofoam disc, 6″ in diameter
  and 1″ thick
48″ of 1⁷⁄₁₆″-wide (#9) orange
  burlap ribbon
24″ of 2¾″-wide (#40)
  plaid ribbon
4 yd of brown curly chenille

3 yellow chenille stems
1½″ x 1½″ each of red, black, and
  white felt
white glue
floral adhesive
yellow spray paint
light pink spray paint

Fig. 7-1 Door Decor project for Mother's Day.

Sprinkle half of the rattan mat lightly with water to soften. Fold over four inches at one edge and hold in place by tying the edge to the center with a chenille stem. Let the mat dry.

Spray the rattan mat with yellow paint. It will probably take three coats to completely cover.

Now spray the Styrofoam disc with pink paint, around the edge and on one side.

To create a simple hairdo, spread glue on the disc surrounding the face and press the brown curly chenille into the glue. Start at the center top and bring curls down over the edge, then back up again. Repeating this three times should cover the edge on one side. Now work to either side of the face. Glue on three or four rows of curls, then add the bangs. Now glue curls on the other side of the face and the edge. If you want to create a different hairstyle, go right ahead.

Cut out eyes from white and black felt and mouth from red, following the patterns in Figure 7-2. Glue the black pupils of eyes onto the white parts. Now glue in position on face, along with the mouth.

Place three pieces of floral adhesive on back side of the Styrofoam disc. Slide the disc up under the folded edge of the mat and center it. Press in place so that the adhesive sticks to the mat. The mat now becomes her hat, with the folded portion as the brim.

Run a gathering thread through the center of the plaid ribbon, then pull it up tightly until it is 6 inches long. Pin and glue the ruffled ribbon in place at her neckline.

Cut the burlap ribbon in half and fold each piece into a bow. Catch the bow centers with the middle of chenille stems. Wrap tightly, leaving 5 inches of stem on each side of bow. Use one end of a stem to attach a bow at top of her hat, twisting it around a piece of the mat. Wrap the other end of the stem around a pencil to make a decorative center. Put the other bow at the center of the neckline ruffle.

Use a 4-inch piece of chenille stem to make a hanger at the back of mat.

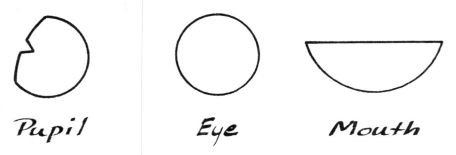

Pupil   *Eye*   *Mouth*

Fig. 7-2 Pattern for lady's eyes and mouth for door hanging.

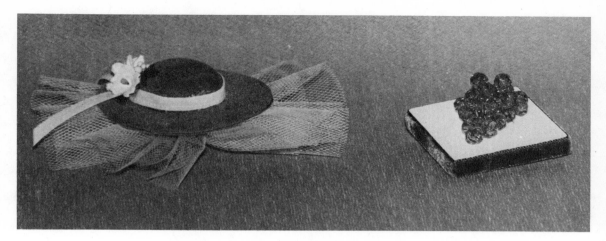

Fig. 7-3 Mother's Day corsage and gift pin.

· Corsage ·

Mother will enjoy wearing the bonnet corsage shown in Figure 7-3 on her special day.

MATERIALS

9″ x 18″ pink net
9″ of 2¾″-wide (#40) fuchsia
   velvette ribbon
9″ of ⁵⁄₁₆″-wide (#1½) pink
   Velvette ribbon
Styrofoam ball, 1¼″ in diameter

3″ x 3″ poster board
small flowers
needle and thread
scissors
corsage pin
white glue

INSTRUCTIONS

Cut the net so one piece is 4 inches by 18 inches, and the other is 5 inches by 18 inches. Use a needle and thread to gather each piece lengthwise through the center. Pull up tightly and knot the thread. Lay the 5-inch piece on top of the 4-inch piece and whip stitch together—I used the different widths for the ruffle to give the corsage more interest.

Cut a 2½-inch circle from the poster board and glue it to the wrong side of the fuchsia ribbon. Cut out. Now glue the poster board side of the circle onto ribbon again, then cut it out. If you do it in this manner, you don't have to worry about matching up the edges.

Cut the Styrofoam ball in half. The remaining piece of fuchsia ribbon should be large enough to cover the half ball. Spread glue over the rounded part of the ball and lay on the wrong side of the ribbon. Press ribbon into the glue and work the ribbon to the edges, smoothing out any wrinkles.

Now glue the crown to the center of your ribbon circle. Can you see a bonnet taking shape?

Glue the narrow pink ribbon around the ball for a hatband and crisscross the ends. Glue the small flowers at this point.

Now glue the hat in the center of the gathered net and let it dry for one hour. Stick corsage pin through the net and your corsage is ready to wear.

· Mother's Day Pin ·

For the pin shown in Figure 7-3, if you don't have a wooden plaque handy, you could substitute a matchbox for the wooden plaque.

MATERIALS

paint brush
white acrylic paint
1½″ x 1½″ wooden plaque
thirty-two 6mm faceted green
   beads

3 tiny green plastic leaves
7″ of ¼″-wide emerald velvet
   ribbon
white glue
pin jewelry finding

INSTRUCTIONS

Cover the plaque with two coats of white paint. Follow the directions on the jar for drying time.

Glue the emerald velvet ribbon around the edge of the plaque.

Following the pattern in Figure 7-4, put a dab of glue on one bead at a time and glue into a cluster. Complete the first layer and allow to dry for a half hour.

Stagger the second layer of beads in the spaces between the beads of the first layer. Allow the glue to dry. You should have three beads for the third layer. Glue these on the center of the bunch, add the leaves at the top, and your grapes are finished. Allow to dry for one hour.

Glue the pin finding onto the top center back of the plaque. Now you have finished your Mother's Day gift.

Fig. 7-4 Pattern for the grape cluster for jewelry pin.

Fig. 7-5 Completed Bonnet Centerpiece.

· *Bonnet Centerpiece* ·

The centerpiece in Figure 7-5 could also be used as a door or wall hanging, without the candle.

MATERIALS

12″ beveled Styrofoam ring
half of a 5″ Styrofoam ball
6½ yd of 2¾″-wide (#40) pink
  patterned ribbon
candle
9″ x 9″ white felt
40 Baggies, sandwich size
10 white chenille stems

1 pink chenille stem
18″ stem wire
pink spray paint
red spray paint
scissors
8 straight pins
white glue

Fig. 7-6 Gathering plastic bag
into a loop to make plastic puff.

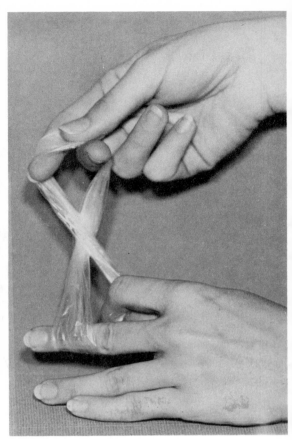

Fig. 7-7 Forming the first figure
eight in the plastic loop.

INSTRUCTIONS

Lay the Styrofoam ring on the white felt and draw around the inside circle. Cut out the circle ½ inch *outside* the marking, as if you were adding a seam allowance. Put aside until later.

To make the plastic puffs, first cut the chenille stems into 3-inch lengths. Now cut the sealed ends off all the plastic sandwich bags.

Slip each hand through the bag, one at either side, and gather into a plastic loop, as shown in Figure 7-6. Twist the loop into a figure eight, as shown in Figure 7-7, then fold in half to form a double loop. Twist the loop again into a figure eight and form another double loop. Put a chenille stem piece through the loop as shown in Figure 7-8 and twist it tightly around the plastic. Cut through the thicknesses of plastic opposite to the stem. Spread and fluff the plastic to complete the puff. Continue until all sandwich bags are formed into puffs.

Start at the edge of the half Styrofoam ball and, using the twisted chenille stem, push a puff into the ball. Put another about 1 inch away. Continue until the rounded part of ball is covered.

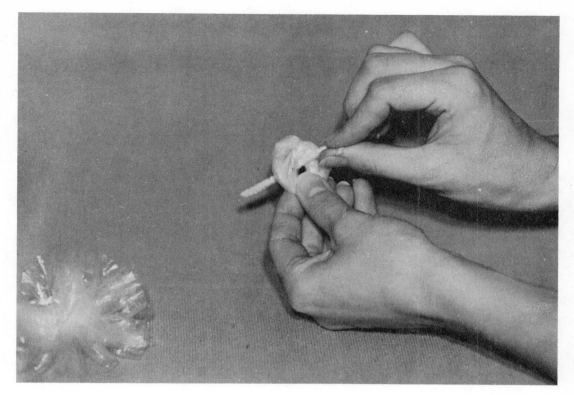

Fig. 7-8 After doubling over to form a loop, making a second figure eight, and folding again, a chenille stem is inserted through the final thicknesses and twisted.

Lightly spray the edges of the plastic puffs with the pink and then the red paints. Set aside to dry.

Cut an 18-inch length from the ribbon for a bow. Using a 4-inch piece of pink chenille stem to fasten at the center, make the bow and set aside.

Cut the ribbon into two equal pieces. This makes for easier wrapping. Use two straight pins to secure one end of the ribbon on the back side of the Styrofoam ring. Pass the ribbon through the center of the ring and begin wrapping. Be sure to overlap the ribbon just enough to cover the Styrofoam. Use all of that piece of ribbon. Repeat with the second piece of ribbon. Pin and glue the ends down.

Cut the stem wire in half. Put one stem wire across the center of the Styrofoam ring, inserting each end into the ring. Put the other stem wire across the first wire at a right angle, inserting the ends also. Put a dab of glue where each wire goes into the Styrofoam.

Lay the puff-covered half ball on top of the wires. Take a 3-inch piece of pink chenille stem and bend it into a U shape. Push into Styrofoam ball from the back at point where the two wires cross.

Spread glue along the edge of a circle of white felt and press it onto the back side of the Styrofoam ring to make a neater looking project.

*Fig. 7-9 Flower Cart (instructions given in Ch. 24)
and Lady Pin Cushion.*

· *Lady Pin Cushion* ·

*This idea, shown in Figure 7-9, was used at a church bazaar and I
thought you would enjoy making it. Try using the L'eggs containers for
making little animals, too. They're great.*

MATERIALS

L'eggs container
1¼ yd of 2¾"-wide (#40) ribbon,
   any color and pattern
7" x 9" poster board
half of a 3" Styrofoam ball
pink spray paint
Bond #527 glue

yellow fake fur
white glue
scissors
two 2" corsage pins
felt-tip pens, black, blue, and red
rouge

INSTRUCTIONS

Use Bond #527 glue to attach the ends of the container parts to each
other. Prop something around it so it will dry straight.

   Following the pattern in Figure 7-10, cut a hat brim, a crown, and

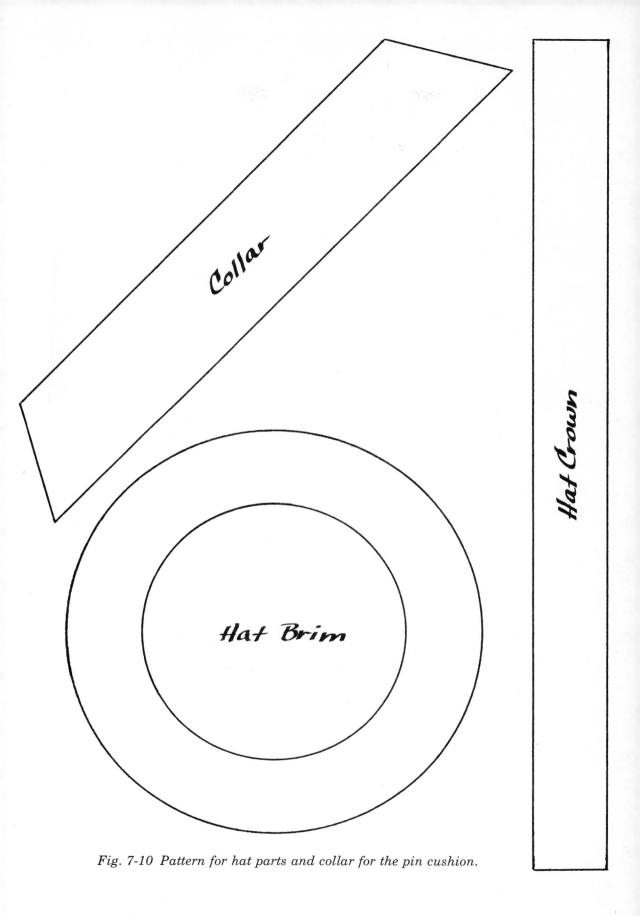

Fig. 7-10 Pattern for hat parts and collar for the pin cushion.

a collar from poster board. Cover each piece on *both* sides with ribbon. For the hat brim, the ribbon will have to be spliced for forming the curves: use white glue for this job. For the collar, glue the ribbon to one side and fold over to other side and glue down. Let dry and trim off the excess. Cover the hat crown on both sides in the same manner.

Using the scraps of ribbon, cut two pieces ¾ inch wide by 5 inches long. Make a bow from each length by folding the ends to center back and gluing down. Cut two small pieces of ribbon, ¼ inch by 1½ inches. Glue one of these to make a loop at the center of each bow.

Spray the half of a 3-inch Styrofoam ball with pink paint. The larger half of the L'eggs container will be the face. So, push the Styrofoam ball, flat side down, ⅛ inch into the container. Run some Bond #527 glue between the ball and container.

Fit the hat brim down over the ball. Then glue the crown of the hat in place. Glue the collar around the neckline. Place one of the bows at collar front and the other bow at center front of hat. It's best to let this dry for one hour.

Decide how far to the front you want the hair. I left 3 inches open in the front, but you could put bangs in this space. Spread glue on container and press fake fur pieces into position and hold.

Using felt tip pens, draw a face following the one shown in Figure 7-9—or do your own thing! Put a tiny bit of rouge on her cheeks and two corsage pins in the top of the hat. She's ready for giving.

❧ 8 ❧

FATHER'S DAY

· A Royal Greeting ·

For father on his special day, why not crown the table with the glittering greeting shown in Figure 8-1?

MATERIALS

2 copen blue 5″ chenille bumps
15 gold 3″ chenille bumps
4 yd white 3″ bump chenille
4 yd brown 3″ bump chenille
8 yd royal blue 3″ bump chenille
2 copen blue 3″ chenille bumps
2 red 3″ chenille bumps
4 gold tinsel stems
2 silver tinsel stems
2 white chenille stems
blue glitter

32″ of 1⁷/₁₆″-wide (#9) white
   Velvette ribbon
5″-diameter Styrofoam ball
Styrofoam disc, 9″ in diameter
   and ½″ thick
4″ x 12″ Styrofoam block, 1″ thick
two 20mm wiggle eyes
flesh-colored spray paint
white glue
scissors
toothpicks

INSTRUCTIONS

The 5-inch Styrofoam ball is the head. Hold in your hands and, with your two thumbs, press in two indentations for the eyes. This also forms the bridge of the nose. Press beneath the bridge to form the base of the nose. Press under the eyes to form cheek bones. Spray the head with flesh-colored paint. Let dry.

Glue two 3-inch brown chenille bumps above the eye sockets to form eyebrows. Place two brown bumps about ½ inch above the eyebrows horizontally to form the hairline. Then place two more brown bumps vertically to form sideburns. Now fill in the top and back of the head to form the hair.

Take two brown bumps and place below the base of the nose, curling the opposite ends up to form a moustache. Place the two red bumps horizontally beneath the moustache to form lips.

The crown is formed by first making a loop from a single gold

Fig. 8-1 A Royal Greeting, centerpiece for Father's Day celebration.

bump: stick both ends of the loop into the Styrofoam in the center front of the head. Then cut a double-bump section, fold in half, and pinch to make a point. Push one end into the Styrofoam next to the loop and the other end ½ inch away. Then continue around, using the same pattern to make a 3-inch-diameter crown. You should use five loops and five doubles to complete the crown.

Cut a 4-inch straight piece of gold tinsel stem. Stick one end into the Styrofoam and bend the other end *over* the top of the point in the double loop. Take another 4-inch piece of gold tinsel and coil it into a circle, leaving ½ inch to stick into the Styrofoam in the center of the gold single loops. Do this all the way around to complete the crown.

Glue the wiggle eyes in place. Take two silver tinsel stems to form the wire-framed glasses. The temple pieces of the glasses should be tucked under the sideburns and the ends inserted into the Styrofoam on each side of the head.

Cut the 9-inch disc in half—you only need half of it for this project. Stick toothpicks into the straight edge of the piece you're using. Spread glue on the 4-inch side of the Styrofoam block. Center the half disc on the block and press the two pieces together. Take the royal blue chenille bumps, form loops and stick into the back of the disc, twist, and press to the Styrofoam. Cover the back of the Styrofoam disc completely. Using eleven white 3-inch bumps, make a V shape down the center front to form the shirt. Push the two 3-inch bumps of copen blue into the Styrofoam to form the knot of the tie. Next take the two 5-inch copen blue bumps and put them vertically down the front to form the rest of the tie.

Fill in the rest of the front and sides with royal blue loops. Take the white chenille stem and shape it to form the lapels. Cut short pieces and push ends into the Styrofoam.

Glue the white Velvette ribbon around the edge of the base. Now fill in the top of the base with white bumps, just as you did the coat. Write "Happy Father's Day" with a thin line of glue along the edge of the base. Sprinkle blue glitter over the lettering.

And there you have it—the perfect greeting for a real prince of a fellow!

FOURTH OF JULY

· Bell Invitation ·

Rally your friends to celebrate the Spirit of '76 with a resounding invitation. (See color section, Figure 5).

MATERIALS

8″ x 8″ poster board
spray adhesive
8″ of 4″-wide (#100) flag ribbon
9″ of ⅝″-wide (#3) red, white, and
   blue striped ribbon
1 red flat bead

2″ of #28 wire
red or blue felt-tip pen
paper
scissors
white glue

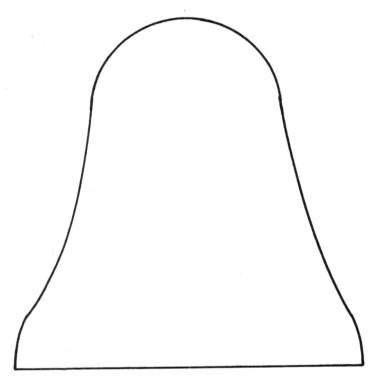

Fig. 9-1 Bell pattern for invitation to the Fourth of July party.

Cut one bell shape out of poster board, following the pattern outline in Figure 9-1. Using spray adhesive, glue the bell to the back of the flag ribbon. Position the bell so that the stars are at the top. When the glue has dried, trim the ribbon to match the bell shape. Make a second bell the same way.

Put the two pieces together, ribbons on the outside, and hold together by using only a small amount of glue at the top. Glue the bead in place for a bell clapper.

Make a bow using the striped ribbon and fasten it by twisting the wire around the center. Glue the ribbon at the top of the bell.

Print the invitation on paper and glue it inside, to the poster board.

· *Firecracker Favor* ·

This favor, shown in Figure 5 in the color section, is simple but it sparkles!

MATERIALS

4″ of 4″-wide (#100) flag ribbon
Styrofoam dowel, 4″ high and 1″
   diameter

1″ x 1″ blue felt
2″ white chenille stem
white glue

INSTRUCTIONS

Glue the ribbon around the dowel. Cut a 1-inch circle from the felt and glue to the end of the dowel. Glue the chenille stem onto the felt to resemble a fuse.

· *Spirit of Independence* ·

The little panorama in Figure 5, color section, is made in individual sections. You can, of course, vary the arrangement by making several fife players—or whatever you like. Instructions are for three figurines and the Liberty Bell Plaque.

· FIFE PLAYER ·

MATERIALS

1-quart soda bottle
6″ x 9″ blue felt
3″ x 6″ brown felt
1″ x 12″ white felt
1″-diameter Styrofoam ball
3″-diameter Styrofoam ball
red spray paint
pink spray paint
red acrylic paint
8″ white chenille stem

2½ yd single-loop gold braid
6″ x 7″ yellow fake fur
1″ x 1″ black felt
1″ x 1″ red felt
one 6mm red faceted bead
4″ red jumbo chenille stem
straight pins
white glue
scissors
serrated knife

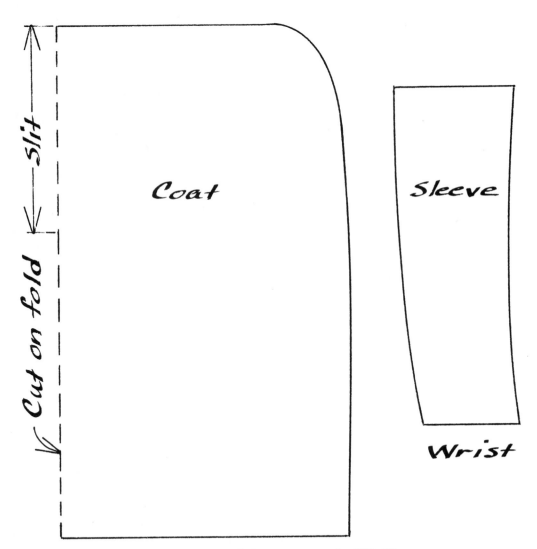

Fig. 9-2 Coat and sleeve pattern for Fife Player.

Spray paint the bottle red. Following the pattern outline in Figure 9-2, cut the fife player's coat and four sleeves from the blue felt. Cut his vest from brown felt, following the pattern in Figure 9-3. Glue gold braid around all edges of the coat, two of the sleeves, and the vest.

While this dries, cut the 1-inch Styrofoam ball in half. Spray both halves and the 3-inch Styrofoam ball with pink paint.

For his eyes, cut two ovals and two small circles from black felt, two small circles from white felt. Assemble and glue these pieces for eyes. When the paint on the 3-inch ball has dried, glue the eyes in place. Use a straight pin to secure the bead in position for a nose. Cut a mouth from red felt and glue in place.

Position one of the rounded ends of the vest at the bottle neck and glue it in place. Position the coat with the slit near the top of the bottle, leaving the rounded corners loose to form coat lapels. Glue the top of the coat around the bottle: the tail of the coat should hang free from the bottle.

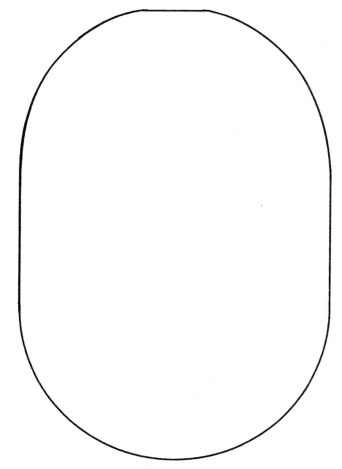

Fig. 9-3 Vest pattern for Fife Player and A Different Drummer.

Holding the two halves of the small Styrofoam ball together, cut a pie-shaped wedge from the straight edge to form fingers. Cut the chenille stem in half and insert one piece into the wrist of each hand. Lay the chenille stem onto one decorated sleeve and glue an undecorated sleeve to it. Repeat for the other arm. This will enable you to shape the arms to hold the fife. Glue the arms in place on the bottle. Secure with straight pins until the glue dries.

Put glue around the mouth of the bottle and push the head onto the bottle. Pin the fake fur onto the head and shape it for hair. Then remove the pins and glue in place. Glue the white felt strip around the head for a bandage and paint a blood stain on it.

Glue the jumbo stem to the hands so your fife player has a fife to play.

· A DRUMMER ·

MATERIALS

1-quart soda bottle	cotton
4″ x 10″ red felt	6mm red faceted bead
5″ x 10″ white felt	two 6mm white faceted beads
2″ x 6½″ blue felt	white glue
1″ x 1″ black felt	white spray paint
12″ gold braid	pink spray paint
12″ red, white, and blue rickrack	straight pins
1″-diameter Styrofoam ball	serrated-edge knife
3″-diameter Styrofoam ball	scissors
red chenille stem	4″ x 7″ poster board
1⅔ yd blue braid	

INSTRUCTIONS

Spray paint the bottle white.

Following the pattern outline in Figure 9-4, cut two coat pieces from red felt and four sleeves from white felt. Glue blue braid around all edges of both coat pieces and the two front sleeve pieces.

While the glue dries, cut the 1-inch ball in half. Spray both halves and the 3-inch ball with pink paint.

Cut two ovals and two circles from black felt, and two circles from white felt, for eyes. Assemble and glue these together. When the paint has dried on the large ball, glue the eyes in place. Use a straight pin to secure the red bead in position for a nose. Cut a mouth from the red felt and glue in place.

Position the armholes in the coat pieces. Fasten in place by gluing at the front and back neckline and around the waist.

Hold the two halves of the small Styrofoam ball together and cut out a pie-shaped wedge to form fingers. Cut the chenille stem into four 3-inch pieces. Insert one stem piece into the wrist of each hand and set the other two stems aside. Lay the chenille stem on the decorated

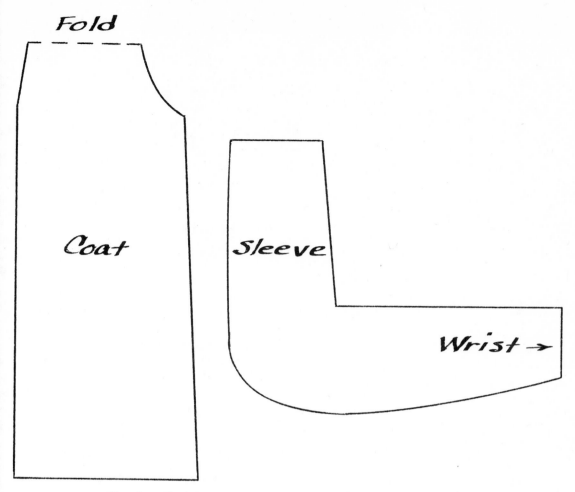

Fig. 9-4 Coat and sleeve patterns for A Drummer and A Different Drummer.

side of one sleeve and glue an undecorated sleeve to it. This gives the sleeve body, so you can shape the arms. Glue the arms to the bottle in position under the coat. Hold in place with pins until the glue dries.

Put glue around the mouth of the bottle and push the head onto the bottle. Shape cotton around the head for hair and glue it in place.

To make the drum, cut out two 2-inch circles from the poster board. Also cut a strip of poster board 1¾ by 6½ inches. Make a tube from the strip; overlap the edges ¼ inch and fasten with glue. Glue one circle to each end of the tube. Cover the side of the tube with blue felt. Trim the edges of the drum with the red, white, and blue rickrack. Glue both ends of the gold braid over the seam in the drum. Slip the braid over the drummer's head and glue the drum in place.

Cut the red chenille stem in half and put a white bead on one end of each piece for the drumsticks. Glue them into the drummer's hands so he can play the beat of freedom.

Fourth of July · 59

MATERIALS

1-quart soda bottle
14″ x 14″ blue felt
3″ x 7″ white felt
1″ x 1″ black felt
3″ x 7″ red felt
1⅔ yd red rickrack
15″ gold single-loop braid
15″ red, white, and blue rickrack
1″-diameter Styrofoam ball
1¼″-diameter Styrofoam ball
3″-diameter Styrofoam ball

blue chenille stem
6″ x 7″ red fake fur
three 6mm red faceted beads
3″ x 15″ poster board
black spray paint
pink spray paint
straight pins
scissors
white glue
serrated-edge knife

INSTRUCTIONS

Spray paint the bottle black.

Following the pattern outline in Figure 9-4, cut two coat pieces and four sleeves from blue felt. Cut a vest from the white felt, using the pattern in Figure 9-3. Glue the red rickrack around all edges of both coat pieces and around the edges of two sleeves. Glue 3 inches of gold braid along the curved edge of the vest.

While this dries, cut the 1-inch ball in half. Paint the halves and the 3-inch ball pink.

Cut two ovals and two small circles from black felt, and two small circles from white felt, for eyes. Assemble and glue these pieces for eyes. When the paint has dried, glue the eyes in place on the large Styrofoam ball. Use a straight pin to secure one bead in position for a nose. Cut a mouth from the red felt and glue in place.

With one rounded end of the vest at the bottle neck, glue it in place. With the larger notch in the coat pieces at the bottle neck, glue down the shoulders and a spot in both front and back at the ends of the coat pieces.

Holding the halves of the small Styrofoam ball together, cut out a pie-shaped wedge to form hands. Cut the chenille stem into four 3-inch pieces. Insert one stem into the wrist of each hand and set the other two stems aside. Lay the chenille stem on one sleeve with the hand at the edge of the sleeve and glue an undecorated sleeve to it. Repeat for the other arm and sleeve pieces. This will enable you to shape the arms. Glue the arms in place on the bottle. Hold in place with pins until the glue dries.

Put glue around the mouth of the bottle and push the head onto the bottle. Pin the fake fur onto the head and shape it for hair. Then, remove the pins and glue the hair in place.

To make the hat, cut two triangular pieces, each 3¼ inches on all sides, from the blue felt and an identical triangle from the poster board. Glue one piece of felt to either side of the poster board. Fold up ¼ inch on each side of the hat to form a brim and glue the corners together. Cut the 1¼-inch-diameter Styrofoam ball in half and cover one half with blue felt. Glue it to the center of the triangle for the hat crown and attach the hat to the head.

To make the drum, cut out two 2-inch circles from poster board and cut a strip of poster board 1¾ by 6½ inches. Make a tube from the strip; overlap the edges ¼ inch and glue. Glue one circle to either end of the tube. Cover the side of the tube with red felt. Trim the edges of the drum with the red, white, and blue rickrack.

Glue both ends of the gold braid to the seam in the drum. Slip the braid over the drummer's head and glue the drum in place. Cut the remaining blue chenille stem in half and put a bead on one end of each piece for the drumsticks. Glue them into the drummer's hands.

· LIBERTY BELL PLAQUE ·

MATERIALS

4½″-high Styrofoam bell
Styrofoam disc, 8″ in diameter
   and 1″ thick
3½ yd red string chenille
4 yd white string chenille
3½ yd blue string chenille
red chenille stem
1 red 5″-bump chenille

3 yd red 1″-bump chenille
6″ of 4″-wide (#100) flag ribbon
28″ of 1⁷⁄₁₆″-wide (#9) red, white,
   and blue striped ribbon
diamond dust
scissors
white glue

INSTRUCTIONS

Cut the red, white, and blue striped ribbon in half. Spread a thin line of glue on cut ends of this ribbon and on ends of flag ribbon. The glue will keep the ribbon from unraveling. Set aside to dry.

Cut the Styrofoam bell in half. Spread white glue on the top of the bell. Starting on the left side of the glued area, press the blue string chenille into the glue. Continue around the outside edge of the top until you are back at the starting point: do *not* cut the string chenille. Continue pressing rows of string chenille into the glue, adjacent to the last row, working toward the center of the top. When the top is covered, cut the chenille to the correct length.

Spread glue on the top third of the rounded surface. Starting at the top left side, press the red string chenille into the glue making a row from left to right, adjacent to the blue top. At the top right side bend the chenille sharply and press another row into the glue snugly against the first row, moving from right to left. Continue until you have fifteen rows of red string chenille, then cut the chenille to the proper length.

Next, spread glue over the middle section of the bell. Using white string chenille, press twelve rows into the glue. Do not cut the chenille until the end of the twelfth row. Spread glue over the bottom part of the bell surface and finish covering the outside with blue string chenille. Set aside to dry. After the outside glue has dried, spread glue inside the curved bell surface, covering a strip one inch wide up from the bottom. Press white string chenille into this glue. Spread glue over the bottom of the bell and cover this surface with red string chenille. Allow this glue to dry. The bell's clapper is made by bending the 5-inch red chenille bump in half and pushing the cut ends into the inside of the Styrofoam.

Using a sharpened pencil, carve the dates "1776–1976" in a semicircle near the edge of the Styrofoam disc. Place glue into the grooves of the numbers. Press blue string chenille into the glue and cut the chenille to the proper length after the numbers are formed. Allow to dry. Spread glue over the numbered surface of Styrofoam disc and sprinkle diamond dust into the wet glue. Allow to dry thoroughly.

Cut the red 1"-bump chenille into pieces with two bumps each. Fold each piece in half. Put a dab of glue on the cut ends of the bumps and push the ends into the edge of the Styrofoam disc. The ends should be placed close together near the front of the disc. Continue around the edge of the disc, placing the pieces snugly against each other. Let the glue dry thoroughly after this step.

Glue the striped ribbon onto the back of the disc in position so that 6 inches of ribbon hang below the disc. Spread glue on the flat, cut surface of the bell and press it firmly to the front of the plaque at the center top. Bend a 4-inch piece of red chenille stem in half and lay it across the center of the 6-inch piece of flag ribbon, twisting the stem together in the back. Push the ends of the stem into the Styrofoam at the top of the bell. Use the other 4-inch chenille stem to form a hanger on the back of the plaque.

· Driftwood and Flowers ·

This attractive centerpiece was used by the Haven Beach Club at its annual Fourth of July celebration. Ginny Matthews designed this creation, shown in Figure 5, color section.

MATERIALS

driftwood
24 blue chenille stems
15 red chenille stems
6 white chenille stems
40″ of 4″-wide (#100) red, white, and blue ribbon
16″ of 4″-wide (#100) red gingham ribbon

floral tape
plastic greens
floral adhesive
5 miniature American flags
pencil
scissors
white glue

Using these materials you are to make fifteen five-petaled flowers. Directions here are for one flower. Coordinate the stem colors and ribbon to suit your taste.

To make a flower, cut a chenille stem in half. Make a loop with each half stem of chenille; each loop should measure about 2 inches long and 1 inch wide. You'll use five loops for each flower. Twist the ends together so that 1 inch of each stem is twisted.

Put glue around one side of the loop and press onto the ribbon. Alternate the way you glue the petal loops to the ribbon to get the most out of your material.

When the glue has dried, cut out the flower petals, trimming the material to match the chenille loop. Hold five petals in a bunch at the stem and twist one of the stems around the other four. Wrap the stems with floral tape. Shape the petals.

The stamen is made by wrapping a chenille stem around the pencil. Slip it off and glue to the center of the flower.

Arrange the greens and flowers on the driftwood and use floral adhesive to secure them. Place American flags at various spots among the flowers.

· Candleholders ·

The candleholders shown in color, Figure 5, can be varied in colors to suit any special occasion.

MATERIALS

two 1¼"-diameter wooden rings
two 1½"-diameter wooden rings
two 2¼"-diameter wooden rings
thirty-two ⅝" gold star sequins
sixteen ¼" red star sequins
sixteen ¼" blue star sequins

2 red candles, 1¼" in diameter
red paint
white paint
blue paint
white glue

INSTRUCTIONS

Paint the 1¼-inch rings red, the 1½-inch rings white, and the 2¼-inch rings blue. When the paint dries, glue the white ring to the blue ring and the red ring to the white one.

Glue eight gold stars at even intervals around each blue ring. Alternate gluing the red and blue stars in the center of the gold stars.

Glue eight gold stars around each red ring at even intervals. Alternate red and blue stars in the center of the gold stars.

Be sure the candles you use fit snugly into the rings.

Fig. 9-5 Bicycling with the independence kids.

· Bicycling ·

The independence kids are shown in Figure 9-5, having a minicelebration.

MATERIALS

6"-high bicycle
42" of 7/16"-wide (#2) red, white, and blue striped ribbon
four 3" blue chenille bumps
five 3" red chenille bumps
three 3" white chenille bumps

three 1½"-diameter Styrofoam balls
six 3mm wiggle eyes
miniature American flag
red felt
white felt

INSTRUCTIONS

To make the colorful spokes, cut the ribbon into four 10½-inch pieces. Wrap the lengths of ribbon around the wheel to cover the spokes and glue the ribbon to the wheel.

The independence kids are made by cutting the chenille into single bumps. Using two bumps of the same color, twist together one end and push into a Styrofoam ball. With another bump of the same color, wrap around the other bumps near the neck to form arms. Glue two wiggle eyes in place. With a different colored bump, make a loop and glue in place for a hat. Glue a piece of red felt in place for the mouth.

Set an independence kid on the bicycle seat, with another figure hanging on the back. The third figure waves Old Glory as they all celebrate Independence Day.

·*Fourth of July Picnic*·

What nicer way to celebrate the Fourth of July than with a good, old-fashioned picnic! And with the new art form called "Decotiques," a dry transfer that rubs designs on instantly, you can create a truly original look. Decotiques go on any surface, smooth or rough, so you can select just about any type of picnic basket or thermos. Because the "Independence" motif includes a variety of patriotic scenes, you don't have to follow the theme pictured in Figure 9-6 if you'd rather do your own thing.

MATERIALS

Decotique No. 7: "Independence"   clear varnish or sealer
picnic basket   ½" paint brush
thermos   ⅛"-wide red mastic tape
paper plates, cups, and napkins   scissors
two serving baskets   pencil
white acrylic paint

INSTRUCTIONS

I chose the two large soldiers for the lid of the picnic basket, using some of the small eagles and drums as trim. However, before rubbing on the Decotiques, I first painted a large white square on the lid with fast drying acrylic paint and edged it with a narrow strip of red mastic tape. Once dry, I started applying the Decotiques.

   Please read the instructions on the Decotique package. Remember,

Fig. 9-6 Picnic regalia: baskets, thermos, plates and cups,
with Decotique Fourth of July motifs.

you need to just roughly cut out the area you want to use because only the artwork is released. The steps are simple:

1. Cut from the sheet
2. Position face down (white side not showing)
3. Rub entire area firmly with applicator or any solid object, such as a knife handle
4. Slowly peel off surface paper: if for some reason, such as too light rubbing, the artwork does not release, just return surface paper to original position and rub again
5. Seal with clear varnish or finish

Turpentine-based varnishes and acrylic water-based sealers can go directly on Decotiques. One coat of any of these finishes seals Decotiques. Additional coats can be applied to achieve different effects.

Application of the sealer to both front and back of the paper plates seals them completely and they can be kept as a wall or shelf decoration or just a memento of the event. Use a plain paper plate to protect the surface while eating. As shown in the picture, the figure of George Washington on his horse framed by the plate makes a most attractive plaque.

Other Decotique designs shown in Figure 9-6 are: thermos, Benjamin Franklin; cup, Liberty Bell; napkin, Betsy Ross; basket #1, Eagles and Drums; Basket #2, July Fourth lettering, Eagles and Drums.

HALLOWEEN

· *Eerie Invitation* ·

For a perfectly ghastly invitation to your perfectly ghoulish party, try sending your friends the one shown in Figure 6, color section and Figure 10-3.

MATERIALS

paper bag
toothpick
1″ x 4″ black felt
white chenille stem

black felt-tip pen
scissors
white glue

INSTRUCTIONS

To make the witch's broom, cut ⅛-inch strips along the 4-inch length of black felt. Do not cut all the way across, leaving a ¼-inch border along the other 4-inch side. Glue one end of the toothpick to one end of the border of felt and roll the felt around the toothpick. Glue the end of the felt to secure and then glue a piece of chenille stem around the top of the broom whisks.

 Cut the paper bag to measure 6 inches by 7 inches, then fold it in half to measure 3½ inches by 6 inches. Glue the broom onto the bag at an angle, and write your greeting with the felt pen.

· *Xyla* ·

What a crazy lady to hang on the porch to greet Halloweeners! Figure 10-1 shows Xyla completed.

Fig. 10-1 Xyla, finished door hanging to greet Halloween visitors.

MATERIALS

scarf
pillowcase
long-sleeved sweater
gloves
panty hose
woman's gown and robe
safety pins

red, blue, and black felt-tip
  markers
2 coat hangers
twine
old clothes and nylons
scissors

Draw facial features on one end of the pillowcase. Stuff with old clothes to form the head. Tie the open end of the pillowcase securely at the back of the head with twine.

Put the sweater over a hanger. Stuff the sweater and arms full with old clothes. Tie the bottom of the sweater so nothing falls out. Pin gloves to sleeve ends.

Stuff the panty hose with old nylons and pin to bottom of the sweater to make legs.

Dress the dummy with a gown and robe.

Slip a coat hanger hook through the knot in the back of the pillowcase head. Hook the two hangers together. Tie a scarf on Xyla's head and she's ready for display.

· *Skeleton and Ghost Wall Hanging* ·

You'll have a simply boo*otiful time making the wall or door hanging shown in Figure 10-3 and in the color section, Figure 6.*

MATERIALS

15″ x 20″ orange burlap
10″ x 19″ black burlap
14″ square white felt
2½ yd ⅞″-wide (#5) white burlap ribbon
3½ yd 1″-wide black ribbon
1″-diameter Styrofoam ball
12 opaque white dog bone beads
nine 7mm x 6mm opaque white lantern beads

six 14mm x 7mm opaque white fluted beads
two 5mm wiggle eyes
16″ wooden dowel
orange paint
waxed paper
white glue
scissors
black felt-tip pen

INSTRUCTIONS

Paint the dowel orange and let it dry.

Place the orange burlap on waxed paper. Fold over an inch of cloth along one 15-inch length and glue along the edge. Insert the dowel into this slot. Cut an 18-inch length of black ribbon and tie one end of it to each end of the dowel for the hanger.

Glue the black burlap onto the orange burlap, leaving a 2½-inch margin of orange along each 19-inch side.

Glue white burlap ribbon on the longer edges of the black burlap and glue black ribbon in the center of the white burlap. Glue white burlap on all four edges of the orange burlap and glue black ribbon in the center of the white burlap. Let this dry.

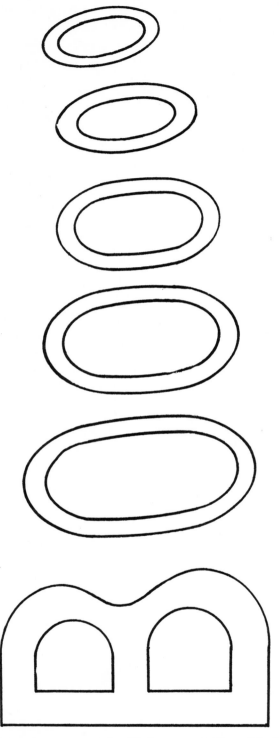

Fig. 10-2 Lettering pattern for Skeleton and Ghost Wall Hanging.

Cut the word "Booooo" from white felt, using the pattern in Figure 10-2, and glue the word across the center of the black burlap.

To reconstruct the skeleton, use dog bone beads as the arms and legs; use lantern beads as the joints and neck bones; use fluted beads for the ribs. Glue the bones in place above the "Booooo." Cut the Styrofoam ball in half and flatten one half slightly. Glue the skull into place and mark the sockets with the black felt pen.

To make the ghost, cut a 4-inch strip of white felt. Cover the other half of the Styrofoam ball with the large piece of white felt and tie the neck with the cut strip. Cut two holes and glue the eyes in place. Glue the head and the edges of the ghost's gown to the black burlap below "Booooo."

Hang up the door piece to welcome the ghouls and goblins.

· Be-Witched ·

What Halloween would be complete without a witch and her brewing cauldron? Make the one shown in Figure 10-3 and in Figure 6 (color section) as a centerpiece for the refreshment table and invite all the goblins and ghosts you know. The following instructions are for the witch, then her fiendish friends are made separately to complete the scene.

· WITCH ·

MATERIALS

Styrofoam block, 9″ wide, 12″ long and 1″ thick
3″-diameter Styrofoam ball
13″ dowel, ¼″ in diameter
black yarn
42″ of ⅞″-wide (#5) orange burlap ribbon
36″ x 36″ black felt
2″ x 4″ gold felt
polyester Fiberfil or cotton

#28 wire
3″ x 3″ flesh-toned construction paper
10″ x 12″ poster board
flesh-colored spray paint
black spray paint
green felt-tip pen
paring knife
scissors
white glue

INSTRUCTIONS

Spray the Styrofoam block with black paint. When dry, cover the edges all the way around with orange burlap ribbon.

Following the diagrams in Figure 10-4, carve the 3-inch ball with a paring knife to make the witch's head. Then paint the head flesh toned. Cut a mouth and eyes to fit from the black felt and glue in place. Highlight the sunken cheeks with the green felt-tip pen.

From the black felt, cut a 12-inch by 24-inch rectangle for the dress and an 8-inch by 17-inch piece for the cape. Fringe the long sides

*Fig. 10-3 Skeleton and Ghost, Scarecrow, Pumpkin Patch,
Owl's Nest, Be-Witched, and Eerie Invitation.*

of the dress and cape and the short sides of the cape. Glue together the
short sides of the dress to make a seam.

Centering the 13-inch dowel along one long side of the Styrofoam,
glue the dowel upright into the Styrofoam 3½ inches from the center
back edge. Cut 18 inches of wire and wrap the center around the dowel
1 inch from the top, leaving 7 inches on either side of the dowel for
arms. Slip the dress over the dowel with the fringed edge down. Shape
the dress and gather it below the wire to make a waist. Secure with a
short length of black yarn.

Use the pattern in Figure 10-5 to cut two hands from the flesh-

72 · *How to Make Party and Holiday Decorations*

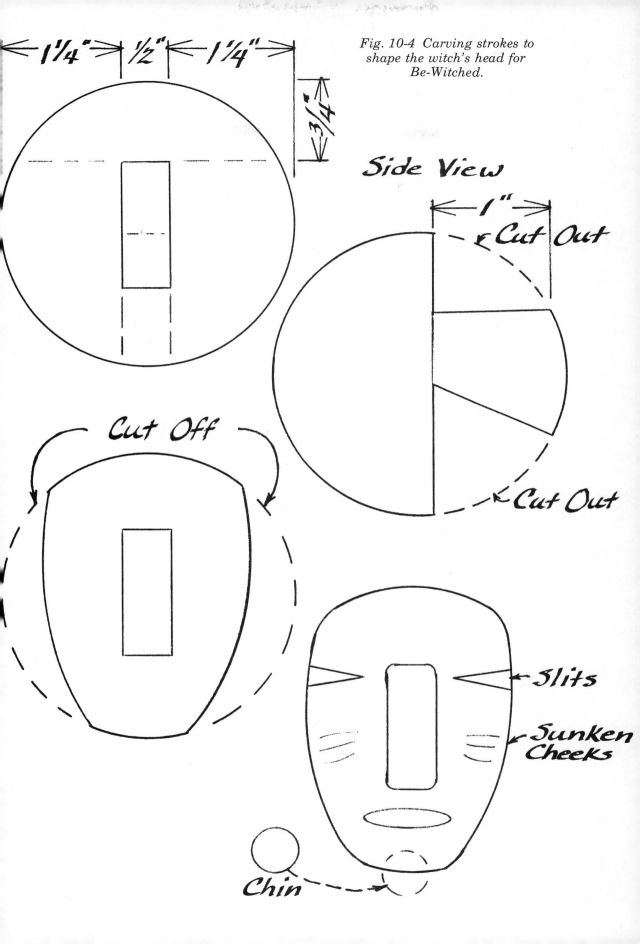

$1\frac{1}{4}"$ $\frac{1}{2}"$ $1\frac{1}{4}"$ $\frac{3}{4}"$

Fig. 10-4 Carving strokes to shape the witch's head for Be-Witched.

Side View

$1"$

Cut Out

Cut Out

Cut Off

Slits

Sunken Cheeks

Chin

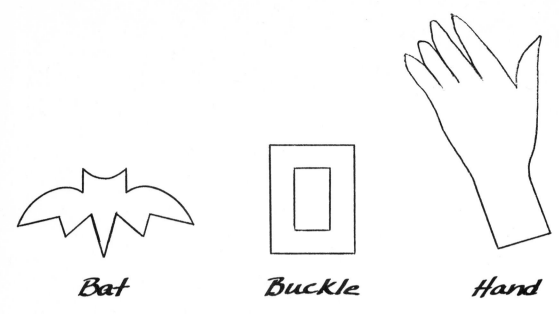

Fig. 10-5 Patterns for bat, buckle, and hand for Be-Witched.

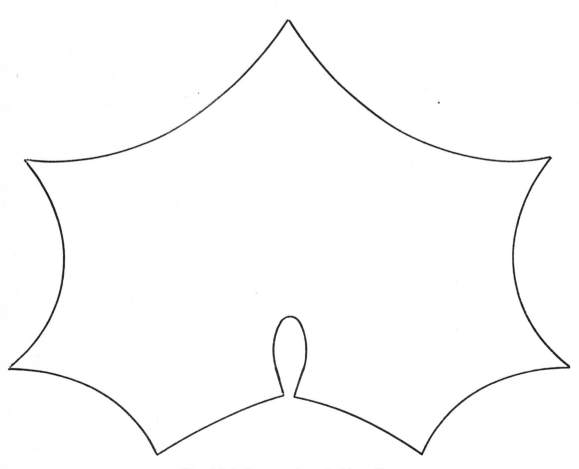

Fig. 10-6 Pattern for witch's collar.

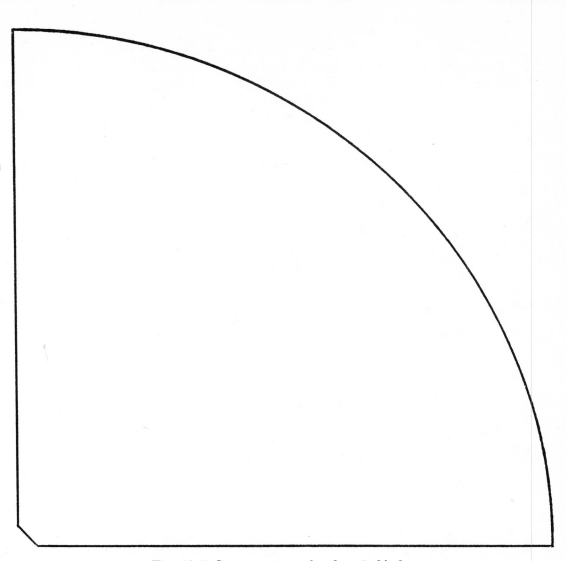

Fig. 10-7 Crown pattern for the witch's hat.

toned paper. Color in nails and veins with the green pen. On the straight edge of the cape, fold over 1 inch and glue. Place hands at either end of the fold. Starting at each end of the wire, fold the cape over the wire. Work toward the dowel from both hands. Form a hump with the excess material at the witch's back.

Cut a bodice piece 3 by 2 inches from black felt. Glue the bodice to cover the wire at the waist. Cut a bat (Fig. 10-5) from gold felt and glue to the bodice.

Using the pattern in Figure 10-6, cut two collars from the felt and one from poster board. Glue one felt collar to either side of the poster board. Slip the collar around the dowel and glue together at the slit. Shape the collar to stand up.

From the black felt, cut one cone-shaped hat from the pattern in Figure 10-7, plus two circles—each with a 5½-inch diameter. Cut one

5½-inch circle from poster board. Glue one felt circle to either side of the poster board circle. Form a cone shape from the felt hat and glue along the straight edge. Glue the cone to the center of the felt circle. Cut a belt buckle (Fig. 10-5) from gold felt and glue to the hat.

Place glue on the neck of the dowel and push the Styrofoam head onto it. Glue Fiberfil or cotton around the head for hair. Glue the hat in place, rolling the front brim down slightly.

· OF CAULDRONS AND SINISTER THINGS ·

MATERIALS

3″-diameter Styrofoam ball	12″ dowel, ¼″ diameter
3″ x 8″ black felt	1½ yd yellow rug yarn
1″ x 1″ green felt	3″ x 3″ cardboard
half of a 5″-diameter Styrofoam ball	plastic autumn leaves
	miniature black cat
4″ x 4″ orange felt	orange spray paint
3″ x 5″ brown felt	black spray paint
polyester Fiberfil or cotton	scissors
10″ of #18 stem wire	white glue
2″ x 4″ poster board	

INSTRUCTIONS

Use the 3-inch Styrofoam ball to make the pumpkin. In order to form ridges, press the ball against the edge of a table at even intervals. Paint the ball orange. When dry, cut a mouth, a nose, and eyes from the black felt and glue the features in place. Cut a stem from green felt and glue in place.

To make the witch's brew, cut two or three strips from the brown felt to resemble logs. Cut a circle of fire from the orange felt. Glue the fire on top of the logs and then glue in place in front of the witch. Spray the half Styrofoam ball with black paint. When it dries, glue the center of the curved surface onto the fire. Cut eight cauldron legs from black felt and four from poster board following the pattern in Figure 10-8. Glue one felt leg to either side of each poster board leg. Glue these in position around the pot. Glue Fiberfil or cotton to the pot for smoke and glue the stem wire in place for the pot handle.

To make the broom, paint the 12-inch dowel black and let dry. Cut off 4 inches of yellow yarn and wrap the rest around the 3-inch by 3-inch cardboard. Carefully slip the yarn off and secure it an inch from one end with the 4-inch length of yarn. Cut the loops on the opposite end. Place glue on one end of the dowel and push it into the center of the yarn. Make sure the yarn is tied snugly around the end of the broomstick, then glue the other end to one of the witch's hands.

Affix the black cat near the broom on the base; add the pumpkin on the other side of the cauldron. Scatter leaves around the base and use a drop of glue to secure them in place. Party time!

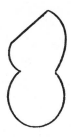

Fig. 10-8 Pattern for the cauldron legs in Be-Witched.

· Pumpkin Patch ·

The easy-to-make pumpkin nest shown in Figure 10-3 and in color (Fig. 6) makes a delightful gift for any autumn occasion.

MATERIALS

two flat rocks
bark
assorted dried flowers
½" x ½" green felt
orange paint
yellow paint

black felt-tip pen
small brush
scissors
glue
waxed paper

INSTRUCTIONS

Lay the rocks on waxed paper and paint them orange. When dry, turn them over and paint the other sides.

Choose the nicest sides for the pumpkin faces. Use the black felt-tip pen to draw outlines on each for the eyes, nose, and mouth. Fill in the outlines with yellow paint. Let dry. Then paint a section of the eyes black with the felt-tip pen. Make the vein lines in the pumpkin with the black pen also.

Cut a small piece of green felt to glue on top of each for stems. Glue the two pumpkins in position on the bark, then add some dried flowers.

This makes a nice party favor or gift for a friend.

· Owl's Nest ·

A hoot owl perched in a tiny nest, whence he surveys the party scene—he's easy and fun to make, shown in Figure 10-3 and in color (Fig. 6).

MATERIALS

2 hickory nuts or acorns
1" x 6" orange burlap
two 10mm wiggle eyes
2" x 2" poster board
sphagnum moss

floral adhesive
¼" x ¼" gold felt
2 large pine cone petals
2 small pine cone petals
white glue

INSTRUCTIONS

Join the two hickory nuts or acorns together, using a small piece of floral adhesive.

Glue wiggle eyes in place on the "head" nut. Then glue the two small pine cone petals into position for the ears. Cup the large pine cone petals *toward* the nut at each side and glue into place for the owl's wings. Cut a small triangle from gold felt and glue on for a nose. Set aside to dry.

Cut a 2-inch circle from the poster board.

Pull all the thread from the burlap, unraveling it all. To make the nest, the threads are glued in a circle around the edge of the poster board. First, glue three threads, one on top of another, then let them dry for a few minutes. Continue gluing the threads until you have built up a one-inch-high nest.

Now you are ready to glue your owl in the nest. Place the sphagnum moss in the nest and hold in place with glue.

This little owl's nest makes a great place-card holder.

· *Scarecrow* ·

Our cute little scarecrow, shown in Figure 10-3 and Figure 6 in the color section, makes a great favor for the Halloween party.

MATERIALS

1¼"-diameter Styrofoam ball
4" x 5" beige burlap
12" of 1⁷/₁₆"-wide (#9) orange
   burlap ribbon
2 yd orange Swistraw or raffia
12" of ⅞"-wide (#5) orange
   polka-dot ribbon
orange chenille stem
3" x 5" black felt

¼" x ¼" red felt
Styrofoam disc, 3" in diameter
   and 1" thick
sphagnum moss
white glue
6 straight pins
pencil
4" x 4" cardboard

INSTRUCTIONS

To make the legs, cut two pieces of orange burlap ribbon, each 3 inches long. Spread a thin line of glue along one 3-inch edge of one piece. Roll it into a tube around a pencil, pressing the glued edge to the other edge on the opposite side of the ribbon. Be careful not to glue it to the pencil. Hold together for a few minutes. Repeat for the other leg.

Now cut the jacket from the beige burlap following the pattern in Figure 10-9. Fringe ¼ inch at the ends of the sleeves and at the bottom edge of jacket. Fold over at the shoulder line and glue underarm and side seams. Keep the sleeves and the bottom open.

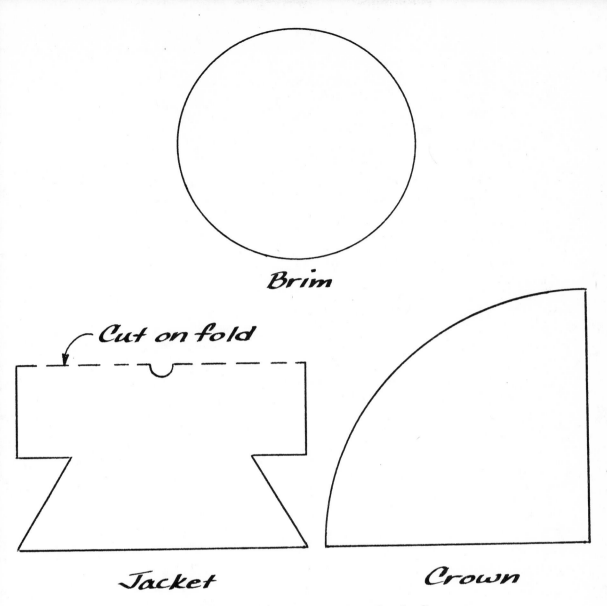

Brim

Cut on fold

Jacket

Crown

Fig. 10-9 *Jacket and hat parts patterns for the Scarecrow.*

Using the hat patterns in Figure 10-9, cut one brim and one crown from the black felt. Roll the crown into a cone shape and glue the edges together. Put glue on the bottom of the crown and place it in the center of the hat brim. Let this dry. Now cut a piece of orange Swistraw or raffia and glue around the hat for a hatband.

Wrap a 40-inch length of Swistraw or raffia five times around the cardboard piece. Very carefully slip it off the cardboard and tie at the center with a small piece of Swistraw. Do this three times.

Stuff one bunch of Swistraw into each of the burlap leg tubes, leaving an inch stick out at one end. Put glue on the other end of each tube and slip them up into the jacket bottom, forming the legs. Cut two 4-inch pieces of chenille stem and push down into each leg, leaving ½ inch stick out below the Swistraw.

Take the other bunch of Swistraw and push through the sleeves in the jacket, leaving ½ inch stick out each sleeve. Glue the rest of the sleeve opening shut so that the arms will stay in place.

Cut a 1-inch piece of chenille stem and push halfway into the Styrofoam ball. Put glue on the exposed end of the stem and slip into the top of the jacket at the neckline.

Cut small triangles for eyes from the black felt. Cut a small triangle from the orange ribbon for a nose and a mouth from red felt.

Glue the eyes, nose, and mouth into place. Glue and pin the hat to the head, crumpling the edges so that it suits our scarecrow.

Cut a piece of burlap ribbon ⅜ inch wide and 6 inches long, then glue around the neck for a scarf. Cut three patches from the polka-dot ribbon and affix at appropriate spots on his garments.

Glue the polka-dot ribbon around the edge of the Styrofoam disc. Spread glue on top of the disc and press the sphagnum moss into it.

To attach the scarecrow to the disc, push the chenille stems sticking out his pantlegs into the Styrofoam. Make a tiny bow from remaining burlap ribbon and put in front of the scarecrow.

Several scarecrows in various colors will really add color to your Halloween party table. Enjoy yourself!

11

THANKSGIVING

· *Raffia Doll* ·

For a lovely wall or door hanging you can use throughout the autumn season, make this delightful doll, shown in color Figure 7.

MATERIALS

10″ x 18″ blue felt
12″ x 36″ blue calico fabric
16″ blue yarn
4″-diameter Styrofoam ball
1″ red fringe ball
2″ x 2″ green felt
1″ x 1″ red felt
2 hanks natural raffia
1 hank red raffia
tan spray paint

white glue
straight pins
18″ x 12″ cardboard
pinking shears
scissors
needle and thread
10″ twine
wire cutters
coat hanger

INSTRUCTIONS

Spray paint the Styrofoam ball for the head. While this dries, you may assemble the body. Cut four 6-inch lengths of raffia. Then using the cardboard, wrap *half* of one hank of natural raffia around the 12-inch length and cut it off from the rest of the hank. Carefully slip the raffia off the cardboard and tie 1½ inches from both ends with a 6-inch length of raffia. Cut the looped ends. This piece will be the doll's arms.

Using the other half of the hank and all of the second hank of natural raffia, wrap around the 18-inch length of the cardboard. Carefully slip the raffia off the cardboard and tie 2 inches from one end with a 6-inch length. Cut the loops on the tied end: this is the neck. Do not tie the other end, but cut the loops. Divide the raffia strands under the neck in half: place the arms horizontally under the neck so that half of the strands are under the arms and half are over them. Bring the strands together under the arms and tie snugly with 6 inches of raffia to form a waist.

Now you can dress the girl. Using pinking shears, cut a 1½-inch by 10-inch strip of calico material for her apron bib. Cut a 5-inch by 7-inch rectangle from the calico and scallop the edges along one 7-inch length of material. This is the apron. Scallop one 18-inch edge of the blue felt for the dress. Using a needle and thread, gather the unscalloped 18-inch edge of the skirt and glue it at the waist of the body.

Place the center of the bib strip at the back of the neck and bring the ends of the material forward so that they cross and lie flat against the waist. Glue both ends at the waist. Gather the unscalloped edges of the apron and glue in place over the bib ends at the waist. Using a 10-inch piece of yarn, tie it around the waist and make the bow in front. Cut two 1-inch by ½-inch rectangles from calico and glue on the skirt for patches.

As all this dries, you can complete the head. Wrap half of the red raffia around the 12-inch length of cardboard. Slip the raffia off the cardboard and tie a 4-inch piece of raffia around it 4 inches from one end. Place the tie on the Styrofoam and glue. The 4-inch length of raffia will constitute the bangs, so spread out the strands and glue periodically. Spread out the longer strands to complete her hair and glue in place on the ball.

Cut two teardrop-shaped eyes from green felt and glue in place. Cut a mouth from the red felt and glue it and the red fringe ball nose in place.

Cut a circle with a 6-inch radius from the calico. Sew a running stitch 2 inches from the edge all around the circle and gather for the hat. Place the hat on the head and adjust it to fit. Glue and pin in place.

Cut an 8-inch piece of coat hanger wire. Push one end into the bottom of the Styrofoam ball. Fan out the body raffia at the neck to form a flat surface. Spread glue onto the raffia and push the wire down through the neck and body. Let it dry.

Tie a length of twine around the neck for a hanger.

· Owlish Mail Basket ·

This delightful decoration is also very useful: place on a table in your entrance hall or hang on the front door. The project is shown in Figure 7 in the color section.

MATERIALS

wicker mail basket
2 yards 2¾"-wide (#40) decorative ribbon
2 orange chenille stems
8" x 4" orange felt
3" x 4" Styrofoam block, 1" thick

black felt
gold felt
assorted dried flowers
floral adhesive
white glue
4" x 4" poster board

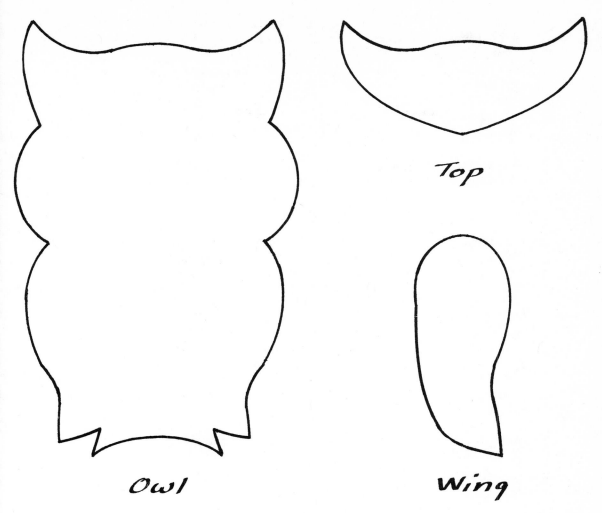

Fig. 11-1 Owl pattern parts for the Owlish Mail Basket.

INSTRUCTIONS

Cut the body of the owl from the orange felt, following the pattern in Figure 11-1. Cut two wings and the top of owl's head from ribbon (Fig. 11-1). Glue these in place on the body. Cut two ¼-inch circles from gold felt and glue in place for eyes. Cut pupils of eyes, nose, and toes from black felt. Glue in place.

Cut another body from orange felt and one from the poster board. Glue the decorated body to the poster board and glue one chenille stem down the other side of the board. Then glue the undecorated body to the poster board. This "sandwich" gives support to the felt owl.

Glue a length of ribbon around the top of the basket just beneath the decorative edge. Make a bow from the remaining ribbon and tie the center with a chenille stem. Attach the bow to the center front of the basket.

Attach the Styrofoam block to the inside bottom of the basket with floral adhesive. Arrange the dried flowers in the basket. Statice is good to use as a filler. Arrange and rearrange the foliage until it's pleasing to your eye. Place the owl in the front of the arrangement.

· Cornucopia ·

A bountiful harvest is the true symbol of Thanksgiving. Shown in color in Figure 8, this cornucopia will make a fine table centerpiece.

MATERIALS

12″-high Styrofoam stack tree
24″ of 1⁷⁄₁₆″-wide (#9) brown polka-dot ribbon
12″ of 1⁷⁄₁₆″-wide (#9) orange and yellow polka-dot ribbon
12″ of 1⁷⁄₁₆″-wide (#9) yellow plaid ribbon
12″ of 1⁷⁄₁₆″-wide (#9) orange satin ribbon
24″ of 1⁷⁄₁₆″-wide (#9) green calico ribbon
15″ of ⁷⁄₈″-wide (#5) brown satin ribbon
4 plastic tea fern picks
2″ x 2″ Styrofoam block, 1″ thick
four 1″ orange fringe balls

1″ brown fringe ball
two 1″ green fringe balls
3½ yd ½″-wide brown flat braid
1⅓ yd of 1⁷⁄₁₆″-wide (#9) orange burlap ribbon
12″ x 11″ brown burlap
11″ x 12″ Styrofoam block, 1¼″ thick
three #16 stem wires
floral adhesive
orange spray paint
white glue
scissors
needle and thread
1½″ corsage pin

INSTRUCTIONS

To make the cornucopia, start with the biggest ring in the stack tree and work toward the small cone. Glue the pieces in order of largest diameter to smallest radius. Curve the structure as you go—that is, don't glue each piece so that it's perfectly centered on the other. While this dries, glue the brown burlap to one surface of the large Styrofoam block. Glue the orange burlap ribbon all around the edges of the block and add the brown braid, placing it in the center of the orange ribbon.

Now the cornucopia should be dry enough to spray with orange paint. Be sure to cover as much of the inside as possible. Let this dry while you make the flowers.

Cut the brown polka-dot ribbon to get two 12-inch lengths. Sew a running stitch ⅛-inch from the edge along one 12-inch length. Pull the gathering stitches tightly and sew the raw edges together. Using a third of a stem wire, make a small hook in one end. Poke the straight end of the stem wire through the gathering and glue the hook in the wire to the material. Make six more flowers from different ribbons the same way. Let them dry for about an hour.

Glue braid around the edge of each cornucopia section. Attach the small Styrofoam block inside the cornucopia 5 inches from the edge with floral adhesive. Glue the cornucopia onto the burlap-covered block, but don't center it.

When the flowers have dried, glue one fringe ball in each flower as the center. Arrange five flowers and the greens, inserting the stems in the block inside the cornucopia. Place two flowers outside, gluing them to the burlap. You may stick the wires in the Styrofoam or cut them off.

Make a bow from the brown satin ribbon and pin it at the top of the cornucopia.

· Pilgrim Children ·

Figure 8 in the color section shows this joyful little scene—pilgrim children frolicking in the sunshine.

MATERIALS

9″ x 12″ brown felt
6″ x 12″ white felt
6″ x 6″ orange felt
two 2″-diameter Styrofoam balls
3″ x 5″ Styrofoam block, 1″ thick
3 yd yellow yarn
four 7mm wiggle eyes
assorted dried flowers
wicker plate or straw mat

sphagnum moss
floral adhesive
red acrylic paint
flesh-toned spray paint
small paint brush
scissors
2 craft sticks
white glue

INSTRUCTIONS

Holding one Styrofoam ball in your hands, press both thumbs about ⅛ inch into the Styrofoam to form eye sockets. At the position for a mouth, press the eraser of a pencil into the Styrofoam about ⅛ inch. Repeat for the other ball. Place them on craft sticks and spray both of them with flesh-toned paint. Let the paint dry thoroughly. After the paint is dry, glue the wiggle eyes in position and paint the mouths red. Set aside to dry.

Following Figure 11-2, cut the following pieces from felt for the girl: one white apron, two white hands, one brown dress, and one brown bow. Also, cut one white 2½-inch-diameter circle for her collar; a white apron string ¼ inch by 5½ inches; one 4½-inch-diameter orange circle for a hat; one brown hatband, ¼ inch by 7½ inches; and two brown sleeves, each 1½ by 1¾ inches.

Take one Styrofoam head and spread glue along the hairline area, where you will place yarn for the girl's hair. Starting at one ear, position, press the yarn into the glue and lay the yarn from front to back,

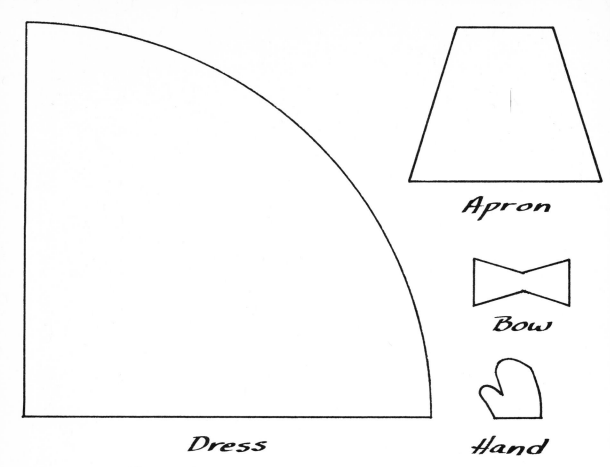

Apron

Bow

Dress

Hand

Fig. 11-2 Pattern for Pilgrim Girl's clothes and body parts.

an inch in length. Turn the yarn to make a loop and press the yarn into the glue from back to front. Continue making one-inch loops up over the head to the other ear position. Cut the yarn. Starting at the crown of the head, press the yarn into the glue making longer loops to hang down over her neck and finish covering the back of the head. Cut the yarn and allow the glue to dry completely.

Roll the brown dress into a cone, overlap ⅛ inch, and glue the seam. The seam will be the back of the dress. Roll the sleeve pieces lengthwise into a tube, overlap ⅛ inch, and glue the seams. Cut the tip of the dress cone. Slip a craft stick up through the opening, extending out ½ inch. Glue the dress to the craft stick. Make a small hole in the center of the white collar and slip the collar down over the craft stick. Place a dab of glue under the collar, front and back, fold down, and glue to the front and back of dress. Place glue on one end of the sleeve, slip under the collar and glue in place. Do both sleeves this way.

Place glue on the wrists of the hands, slip the wrists into the

Fig. 1 New Year's Eve: Clock, Champagne Favors, Gala Invitation,
Father Time

Fig. 2 St. Patrick's Day: St. Patrick's Garden, Leprechaun,
Wall Hanging, Shamrock Favor

Fig. 3 Easter: Easter Rabbit House and Bunnies,
Bunny Favor, Egg Tree, and Jelly Bead Fantasy

Fig. 4 May Day: Maypole Dance, Miniature May Baskets, and Gift Basket

Fig. 5 Fourth of July: Spirit of Independence panorama–Fife Player,
A Drummer, A Different Drummer, Liberty Bell Plaque;
Driftwood and Flowers Centerpiece; Firecracker Favor,
Candleholders, and Bell Invitation

Fig. 6 Halloween: Be-Witched, Skeleton and Ghost Wall Hanging,
Eerie Invitation, Pumpkin Patch, Owl's Nest, Scarecrow

Fig. 7 Thanksgiving: Owlish Mail Basket and Raffia Doll

Fig. 8 Thanksgiving: Pilgrim Children and Cornucopia

Fig. 9 Christmas: Patchwork Candlestick, Patchwork Tree, Li'l Miss

TOP: Fig. 10 Bridal Shower: Sweetheart Centerpiece and Pink Parasol

BOTTOM: Fig. 11 Wedding: Bride and Bridegroom, Wedding Bells

Fig. 12 Wedding: Bell Favor, Book Invitation,
Place Card, Matchbook, and Egg Favor

Fig. 13 Baby Shower: Stork, Playpen Favor, Bonnet Invitation, Baby's
Gift Box

BELOW: Fig. 14 Child's Birthday: Birthday Circus Wagon with Lion, Cake, and Presents; Circus Cage with Tiger and Gorilla

BOTTOM: Fig. 15 Father's Birthday: Owl Clock, Table Setting, and Centerpiece

sleeves with the thumbs up, and glue in place. Glue the apron to the front of the dress. Glue the apron string along the top of the apron, placing the ends to the back and crossing them.

Run a gathering thread around the orange circle, ½ inch from the edge. Pull the thread so that the hat will fit on her head. Knot the thread and glue the hat in place on her head. Glue on the brown hatband to cover the gathering thread, adding the brown bow at the front of the hat. Place glue on the end of the craft stick and push the stick into the Styrofoam head. Set aside to dry.

Cut the following pieces from felt for the boy. Following the patterns in Figure 11-3, cut two white hands, two brown shoes, one brown bow, one brown hat, and one brown shirt. Also, cut one white collar, 2 by 3 inches; two white pant cuffs, 1 by 1¾ inches; four brown pieces, 1½ by 1¾ inches, for arms and legs; one brown buckle, ½ by ¾ inch; one orange buckle center, ¼ by ¼ inch; and one orange hatband, ¼ inch by 5½ inches.

Glue yellow yarn to the remaining Styrofoam head, following the same directions as for the girl's hair, except you do not glue the long hair in back. Let the glue dry thoroughly.

Fold the shirt in half at the narrow part and glue the side seams together. Cut a small hole in the center of the fold at top. Slip a craft stick up through the hole, letting it stick out ½ inch. Angle the stick slightly to one side and glue the shirt to the stick at the neckline.

Slit the collar halfway, starting at the middle of one 2-inch side. Fold the collar, place the slit around the stick, and glue down over the shirt. The slit in the collar will be his front.

Roll the sleeve pieces lengthwise, overlap ⅛ inch, and glue the seams. Roll the leg pieces along the short length, overlap ⅛ inch, and glue the seams. This makes the legs larger than the sleeves. Roll the cuff pieces lengthwise, overlap ⅛ inch, and glue the seams. Allow the glue to dry.

Place glue on one end of a sleeve. Slip the glued end underneath the collar and press into place. Place glue on the wrists, slip into the sleeves, and glue the hands in place. Place glue on one end of leg pieces. Slip these just under the edge of the shirt—one of the legs is to be slipped over the craft stick to hide it from view. Glue the legs in place. Now place glue on one end of the cuffs and glue them to the ends of the legs. Place the legs and cuffs end to end. Do not place the legs inside the cuffs. Next glue the shoes to the bottoms of the cuffs. For the leg that has the craft stick, the shoe will have to be cut in half, with the halves glued to the front and back of the stick.

Roll the hat into a cone, overlap ⅛ inch, and glue the seam. Cut a brown piece of felt to cover the opening at the top of the hat and glue in place. Glue the hatband ½ inch from the bottom of the hat. Glue the buckle and buckle center onto the hatband at the front. Next, glue his hat onto his head.

Place a dab of glue onto the end of the craft stick and push the Styrofoam head down on the stick into position.

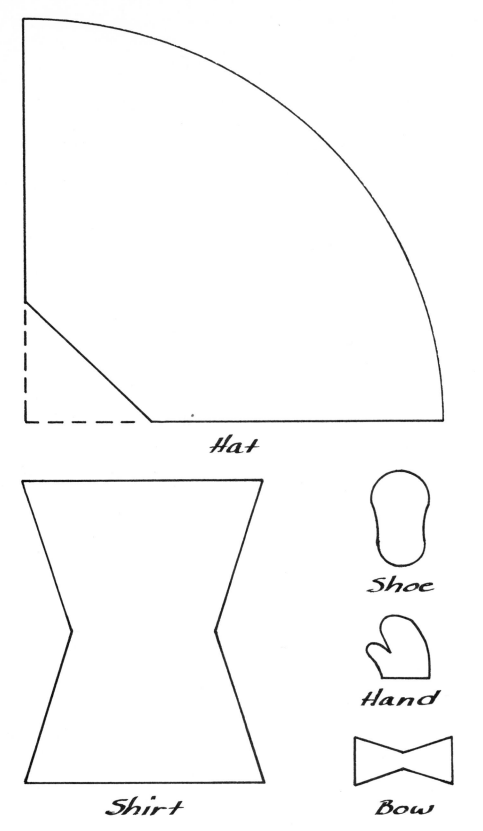

Hat

Shoe

Hand

Shirt

Bow

Fig. 11-3 Clothing and body part patterns for Pilgrim Boy.

Fasten the Styrofoam block to the mat, using floral adhesive. Cover the Styrofoam with sphagnum moss. Push the craft sticks holding the girl and boy through the moss into the Styrofoam. Arrange the dried flowers around the children.

· Pine Cone Figurines ·

· CONE GIRL ·

Instructions are given here for making a girl and a turkey, shown in Figure 11-4, but the idea can be adapted to all kinds of novelty characters. Try your hand at it to see how many variations you can come up with.

MATERIALS

3″-high pine cone
1 orange chenille stem
1 yd yellow yarn
18mm wooden bead head
sprig of statice

6″ of ⅝″-wide (#3) orange
    polka-dot ribbon
1 orange plastic wavy disc
scissors
white glue

INSTRUCTIONS

The smallest part of the cone is the neck for the girl. Glue the wooden bead head at the neck. To make her hair, drape yarn around the face and back of head, gluing it down at the top.

Fig. 11-4 Pine Cone Girl and Pine Cone Gobblers.

Cut a 6-inch piece of chenille stem for the arms. Cut a piece of ribbon ½ inch wide and 5 inches long; glue the ribbon around the chenille stem lengthwise, leaving ½ inch of stem extended beyond each end. Wrap around the cone near the top and shape the unwrapped ends of the stem to form hands.

Glue the disc in place for a hat. Make a bow from 6 inches of remaining narrow ribbon and glue to the top of the hat, covering the hole in the disc. Glue the sprig of statice in the girl's hand.

· PINE CONE GOBBLER ·

MATERIALS

3″-high pine cone
1 yellow chenille stem
1 orange chenille stem

4″ of 2¾″-wide (#40) orange and
yellow polka-dot ribbon
two 7mm wiggle eyes

INSTRUCTIONS

Follow the pattern in Figure 11-5 to trace feathers onto the back of the ribbon; then cut them out. Glue near the large end of the cone, as shown in Figure 11-4.

Cut 3 inches of yellow and 3 inches of orange chenille stem. Twist the two together, one around the other. Shape one end into a small hook to make the turkey's head, shape the length into a graceful curve for his neck, then glue the other end to the narrow part of cone. Glue the wiggle eyes in place. Gobble! Gobble!

Fig. 11-5 Tail feathers pattern for Pine Cone Gobbler.

12

CHRISTMAS

· *Ring Around Angel* ·

There are so many sizes of wooden curtain rings to choose from now. It's a welcome challenge to see what ideas you can dream up for each size. One day in the workshop I decided to try one ring inside another ring. The fit was perfect, and that led to the formed angel shown in Figure 12-1.

MATERIALS

1¼"-diameter wooden ring	white glue
2¼"-diameter wooden ring	green paint
18" red braid	white paint
9" gold braid	½" brush
10" of $5/16$"-wide (#1½) red ribbon	#220 sandpaper
3" x 3" white net	scissors
3 gold star sequins	paper towel
¾"-high miniature angel	toothpick

INSTRUCTIONS

Sand both rings until smooth. Wipe away any dust with a damp towel. Paint the large ring green and the small one white. Let both dry completely.

Glue the small ring inside the large ring. Glue the netting to the back of the green ring. Let dry and trim away the excess netting.

Glue the tiny angel in the center of the ring against the net, with the bottom of the angel snugly against the white ring. Glue the stars over her head.

Beginning at top of ring, apply a thin line of glue in the groove between rings. Place the gold braid directly on the groove. Then glue the red braid over the inside edge of the gold braid. Glue the cut ends of remaining red braid at center top also, making a loop for hanging.

Make a bow with the red ribbon and glue at the top, hiding the seams of the braid.

Fig. 12-1 Ring Around Angel and Green Garden ornaments.

Try this idea with various colors and assorted miniatures. A tree can be interestingly decorated in this manner using a variety of rings you have made.

· *Green Garden* ·

This ornament, shown in Figure 12-1, is very versatile. Try it with other colors of ribbon and flowers. You can dry some flowers and weeds in the fall, spray paint them, and use them in your garden ornament.

MATERIALS

half of a 3½"-high clear plastic
   egg
Styrofoam disc
12 star flowers
plastic greens
12" green bead garland

18" of ⁵/₁₆"-wide (#1½) green
   velvet ribbon
9" gold cord
white glue
scissors
serrated-edge knife

Using a serrated knife, cut the Styrofoam disc in half. Spread white glue on the bottom of the disc and place it in the wide part of the clear plastic egg, flush with the bottom of the ornament. Let it dry thoroughly so that the disc will stay in place.

Starting at the center bottom of the egg, spread glue around the outside edge of the egg. Lay the velvet ribbon into the glue. Then apply glue to the inside lip of the egg and press the beads into it firmly. Lay aside to dry.

Use remaining piece of velvet ribbon to make a bow (*See* Ch. 1, Making a Bow). Put glue on the back of the bow and position at the bottom of the egg in the center.

Break the stems of the star flowers: make three stems 2½ inches long, three stems 1½ inches long, and four stems 1 inch long. Dip the ends of the stems into white glue. Adhere to the disc at the back. Arrange the flowers in half-moon shape.

Cut plastic greens into small pieces. Glue one piece at a time to the Styrofoam disc. Continue until you have covered the disc.

Slip one end of the cord under the beads at the center top. Tie a knot in the end. Your new arrangement is ready for hanging.

· Holly Bead Tree ·

Tiny holly leaves can be used in many ways for Yuletide decorations; one ornament is shown in Figure 12-2.

MATERIALS

4″ x 6″ plastic sheet	6″ gold cord
18 small red plastic holly leaves	scissors
1 large green plastic holly leaf	white glue
embroidery needle	

INSTRUCTIONS

Cut the plastic sheet, following the pattern outline in Figure 12-3. Arrange the red holly leaves on the plastic tree, but do not glue in place until you are pleased with the arrangement. Starting at the top, place four red leaves down the center of the tree. Place three leaves diagonally on each side of the center row, starting at the base tip of the top leaf, (Fig. 12-2). Now place four leaves diagonally in two rows on each side of the center row.

Place the large green leaf at the bottom for the tree trunk. When you are satisfied with the position of the leaves, glue them in place.

Using a needle, punch a hole at the top of the tree. String the gold cord through the hole and knot for a hanging loop.

Fig. 12-2 Holly Bead Tree and Satin Animation ornaments.

· Satin Animation ·

There's no limit to the novelty critters you can make using the basic methods of the next two projects—the cuddly puppy and kitten in Figure 12-2 are only a sample. If you enjoy making these hanging ornaments, you'll want to try some of the satin stand-up figurines in *Christmas Creations,* also published by Chilton.

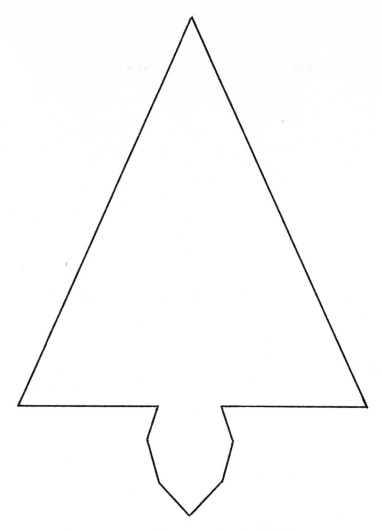

Fig. 12-3 Pattern for the Holly Bead Tree

· SATIN PUPPY ·

MATERIALS

4″ x 4″ gold felt
1″ x 1″ red felt
6″ gold rickrack
3″-diameter green satin ball
14″ gold double-loop braid
¾″ gold triple crown

1 round red flat-back jewel
2 gold flat-back ovals
scissors
pencil
white glue

INSTRUCTIONS

Using the patterns in Figure 12-4, cut out the following: 2 gold felt ears, 2 gold felt eyes, and 1 red felt tongue.

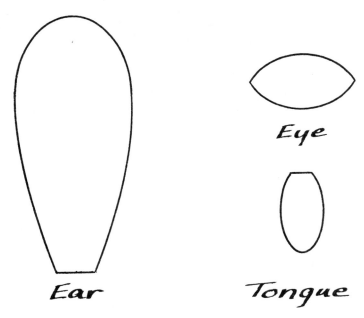

Fig. 12-4 Pattern parts for the Satin Puppy.

Glue gold braid in place along the edge of each ear. While that is drying, glue the rickrack around each eye. Since these are small eyes, it may be easier to fold the rickrack at the pointed ends instead of trying to make it curve around the form.

Remove the hanging ring that comes in the ball. Glue the gold crown over the hole, then glue the ring back into the hole. Place the ears close to the crown as shown in Figure 12-2 and fasten just at the top with a dab of glue.

Glue the two felt eyes in place, then glue an oval jewel onto each felt eye. Position the tongue and glue it only at the top. Glue the red jewel at the top of the tongue.

With a few variations, you can make a companion for this puppy.

· CHRISTMAS KITTY ·

MATERIALS

3″-diameter green satin ball
4″ x 4″ black felt
10″ gold double-loop braid
8″ gold single-loop braid
¾″ gold triple crown
1 round green flat-back jewel

2 teardrop green flat-back jewels
half of a gold tinsel stem
scissors
pencil
white glue

INSTRUCTIONS

Using the patterns in Figure 12-5, cut out the following: 2 black felt ears, 2 black felt eyes, and 1 small black felt circle.

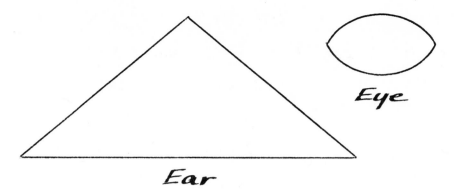

Ear

Eye

Fig. 12-5 Pattern parts for the Christmas Kitty.

Glue a 5-inch length of the gold double-loop braid along the two shorter sides of each cat's ear. Leave the long edges untrimmed. When glue has dried, turn the ear over (trimmed side down) and place your forefinger in the center, pointing at the corner connecting the two shorter sides. Next, roll the felt around your finger and, with a dab of glue, join the remaining two corners. Repeat for the other ear and let these dry.

Now, to trim the eyes, glue the single-loop braid around the black felt eyes starting at the pointed end. This will maintain the teardrop shape.

Remove the hanging ring that comes in the ball. Glue the gold crown over the hole and then glue the ring back into the hole. Now, apply glue to the untrimmed side of one ear and place it close to the crown. Repeat for the other ear.

Glue the two felt eyes in place and then glue a teardrop jewel on each felt eye. Position the small black felt circle to resemble a nose. Then cut the tinsel stem in half and criss-cross the felt nose for whiskers. Glue whiskers on and let dry thoroughly before gluing the round jewel over the tinsel stems.

Now that you have completed two of our favorite satin animals, use your imagination and start a zoo on your Christmas tree.

· *Golden Ball* ·

Select individual picture motifs for the golden ball in Figure 12-6 and make a personalized ornament for each member of the family.

MATERIALS

3″-diameter Styrofoam ball
40″ of ⅝″-wide (#3) green Velvette
   ribbon

5″ x 10″ gold felt
56″ single-loop gold braid
1 package ½″ sequin pins

Fig. 12-6 Golden Ball and Sweet Memory decorations.

1 strand 3mm pearls 6mm pearl corsage pin
3-ring pearl crown scissors
straight pins 4 gummed paper pictures

INSTRUCTIONS

Using the pattern in Figure 12-7, cut four pieces from gold felt. Apply glue to the edges of one piece of felt. Lay it onto the Styrofoam ball. The felt will stretch and conform to the ball shape. Pull it gently until each pointed end is at either end of the ball. You might want to pin it in a few places to help hold the felt down. Use this process for all four pieces

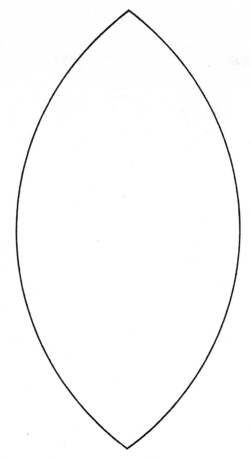

Fig. 12-7 Pattern for the felt ovals for Golden Ball.

of felt. The edges of the felt should meet. The points of felt will all come together at the top and bottom of the ball.

Cut the ribbon into four 5½-inch pieces. Spread glue along the seams where the pieces of felt meet. Using a straight pin, fasten the ribbon at the top of the ball and lay the ribbon into the glue along the seam. Pin the ribbon on the bottom also. Repeat for each seam.

Now you're ready to glue the single-loop braid to each side of the ribbon. Spread glue along the edges of the ribbon and lay the braid into it.

Put a straight pin through each pearl and at intervals of ½ inch, push the pin through the single-loop braid into Styrofoam ball. Trim all braid edges in this manner.

Take a 6-inch piece of ribbon and cut it lengthwise into four strips ⅛ inch wide. Put the cut ends of one ribbon on top of ball and attach it to the Styrofoam by pushing a straight pin through the ribbon. Slip the ribbon through the center of three-ring pearl crown and glue the crown to the top of the ball.

Christmas · 99

Fold the other ⅛-inch-wide strips of ribbon in half. Slip the 6mm pearl onto the corsage pin. Push the pin through the fold in the strips of ribbon and push the pin into the ball at the center bottom. Now you have a fringelike rim on the bottom of your Christmas ball.

Put one picture in each section of the ball. Secure them to the ball by pushing a pin through a small pearl and then into the ball. Depending on the size of your pictures, secure each with fifteen to twenty pins.

· Sweet Memory ·

What a nice way to keep some Christmas memories. The one shown in Figure 12-6 was our family's last card from "Mom Kesler." We treasure it very much.

MATERIALS

Christmas card
3⅝" x 5" x 1⅛" plastic dome
16" gold braid
16" of 2"-wide (#16) gold Velvette
   ribbon

1½"-diameter gold ring
diamond dust
scissors
pencil
white glue

INSTRUCTIONS

Trace the shape of the plastic dome onto the back of the Christmas card scene. Cut out the picture along this line.

Place glue on the card at spots to be highlighted. On my card, I used the snow areas on the buildings and ground. Then sprinkle diamond dust onto the glue. Let dry before proceeding.

Spread a thin line of glue around the edge of the card and press the plastic dome gently in place. Then glue gold braid around the edge of the dome.

Put one end of the gold velvette ribbon through the gold ring and glue down one inch to hold the ribbon on the ring. Cut a V into the other end.

Glue the dome-covered card in the center of the ribbon. This makes a lovely hanging for near the door. Do a group like this.

· Blue and Green Ball ·

Medallions and beads add the distinctive touch to this special Yule creation shown in Figure 12-8.

Fig. 12-8 Wormy Apple, Blue and Green Ball,
and Pretty Pink Egg ornaments.

MATERIALS

4″-diameter Styrofoam ball
7″ x 14″ blue felt
1⅓ yd ⅝″-wide (#3) green velvet
   ribbon
9″ gold cord
1 package 1″ straight pins
1 package gold sequins
66 blue 6mm beads
1 strand 3mm pearls

six 1″-diameter gold paper
   medallions
ten ½″-diameter gold paper
   medallions
1 pearl-headed corsage pin
scissors
pencil
tape measure
white glue

INSTRUCTIONS

Cut five pieces of blue felt following the pattern outline in Figure 12-9.
Apply white glue to the edges of one piece of felt and lay on the
Styrofoam ball. Stretch and form the felt to fit the ball. Pull gently
until each pointed end is at the top and bottom points on the ball. Press
the felt to the ball. You may want to pin the felt in a few places to hold

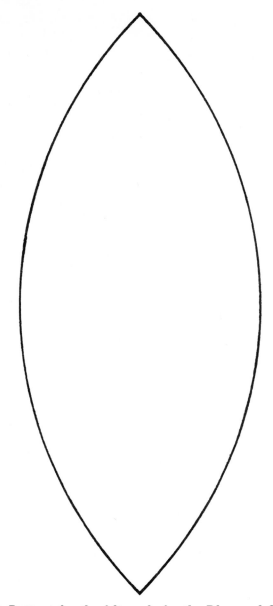

Fig. 12-9 Pattern for the felt ovals for the Blue and Green Ball.

it in place until the glue is dry. Continue placing the pieces of felt to cover the ball. The edges of the felt pieces should meet and the points of the felt should all come together at the top and bottom of the ball.

Measure the distance halfway around the ball. Cut the green velvet ribbon into five pieces equal to the length measured. Spread glue onto the seams where the pieces of felt come together. Fasten one piece of ribbon at the top of the ball with a straight pin. Lay the ribbon over the glued seam and pin at the bottom of the ball. Smooth out the ribbon and be sure that the glue is under all the edges. Continue placing ribbon until all seams are covered.

To decorate the edges of the ribbon, place a 3mm pearl and then a gold sequin onto a straight pin. Stick the pin through the edge of the ribbon and into the Styrofoam ball. Place the pearl, sequin, and pin combinations ½ inch apart, on both edges of the ribbon. Continue until all ribbon edges are decorated.

Spread white glue on the back of a *large* gold medallion. Place a large medallion in the center of each felt section and one over the ends of the ribbon at the bottom of the ball. Place a 3mm pearl and then a 6mm blue bead onto a straight pin. Stick the pin through the center of the medallion into the Styrofoam ball. Now place pearl, bead, and pin combinations through each point of the medallion. Continue until all medallions are decorated.

Spread white glue on the back of the small gold paper medallions. Place these medallions halfway between the large medallions and the ends of the felt sections, both top and bottom. Place a 3mm pearl and then a 6mm blue bead onto a straight pin. Stick the pin through the center of the medallion. Place a pearl, bead, and pin combination in the center of all of the small medallions.

Tie the ends of the gold cord together, thus making a loop for hanging the ball. Glue the loop to the top of the ball. Make a single-loop bow from the remaining velvet ribbon. Attach to the top of the ball by pushing the corsage pin through the center of the bow and into the ball.

· *Pretty Pink Egg* ·

This unusual ornament is shown in Figure 12-8.

MATERIALS

3 packages pink leaf sequins	22″ green velvet tubing
8 green velvet leaves	2″ corsage pin
3″-high Styrofoam egg	scissors
1 box ½″ straight pins	white glue

INSTRUCTIONS

Starting at the smaller end of the egg, glue and pin three sequins so that they lie flat and overlap just on the end of the Styrofoam. Place all of the sequins so that no Styrofoam is seen. Cover the rest of the egg, using two pins to fasten each leaf sequin. Position the sequins with the point of the leaf downward in rows around the egg. Overlap each row about one-third over the preceding row. Continue until the egg is completely covered.

Glue and pin the eight velvet leaves in a circle at the top, or big end, of the egg.

Use 12 inches of green velvet tubing to make a bow. Tie the ends of the remaining pieces of tubing together. Push the corsage pin through the knot and then through the center of the bow. Put a dab of glue on the pin and push the pin into the top of the egg.

Your Pretty Pink Egg is now ready for display.

· Velvet Fruit ·

Here are two possibilities for velvet tubing fruit. Styrofoam can be pressed with your fingers to resemble any fruit shape, so when you have mastered the apple (Fig. 12-8) and the tangerine—try a banana.

· TANGERINE ·

MATERIALS

2½ yd orange velvet tubing
2″-diameter Styrofoam ball
2 green velvet rose leaves
2″ corsage pin

16″ gold cord
1 dozen straight pins
scissors
white glue

INSTRUCTIONS

Flatten a small spot on the ball by rolling and pressing it against a hard surface. This is the bottom. To begin covering the ball, put a row of glue on the *top* of the ball. Then lay the tubing in the glue and begin wrapping it around the form. Continue, placing a row of glue on the Styrofoam first, then laying the tubing along the glue. Pin the tubing at random to prevent slipping. Cover the entire ball.

Place a dab of glue on the stems of the velvet leaves. Push the stems into the Styrofoam at the top. Tie a small bow in the center of the gold cord and push the corsage pin through the knot in the bow. With a dab of glue on the point of the pin, push it into the center top of the ball. Tie the two loose ends.

· WORMY APPLE ·

MATERIALS

3 yd red velvet tubing
3″-diameter Styrofoam ball
2 green velvet rose leaves
1 green chenille stem
two 5mm wiggle eyes
2″ corsage pin

24″ gold cord
1 dozen straight pins
pencil
scissors
white glue

Press the end of your thumb into the Styrofoam ball to make a depression ¼ inch deep. This is the top. Opposite this, flatten a small part of the ball by rolling and pressing it against a hard surface.

Place a dab of glue into the depression at the top and a row of glue around the edge of the depression. Start wrapping the velvet tubing, with the end in the depression, and then lay it on the row of glue. Do not cut the tubing—leave it in one strand. To cover the ball, put a row of glue on the Styrofoam first, then lay the velvet tubing into the glue. Do one row of glue at a time. Continue until the ball is completely covered. It is helpful to pin the tubing at random in order to prevent slipping.

Put a dab of glue on the stems of the velvet leaves. Push the stems into the Styrofoam at the top. Tie a small bow in the center of the cord and push the corsage pin through the knot in the bow. Put glue on the point of the pin and push it into the center top of the ball. Tie the two loose ends together for the hanger.

To make the worm in the apple, wrap the chenille stem around a pencil to form a coil. Glue the wiggle eyes on one end of the coil. Put a dab of glue on the other end of the stem and insert into the top of the apple.

Now—try a banana!

· Dream Wreath ·

The Dream Wreath in Figure 12-10 is done in green and white. You might like to try making it in a variety of color combinations, as Decorative Puff is so easy to work with.

MATERIALS

1 package green Decorative Puff
ten 1¼"-diameter white satin
   balls
2 yd of 1⁷/₁₆"-wide (#9) white
   ribbon

two sprays of white leaves
12"-diameter Styrofoam ring
white chenille stem
4 green chenille stems

INSTRUCTIONS

The Decorative Puff I used comes in 12 by 24 inch sheets. Divide into two pieces by pulling apart and using it half thickness. (The package will make two wreaths.) Cut one piece in half lengthwise so you have two 6 by 24 inch pieces.

Cut three green chenille stems into 3-inch pieces. Bend each into a U shape.

Lay one piece of Decorative Puff along half of the Styrofoam ring.

Fig. 12-10 Dream Wreath, decorated with satin balls.

Fig. 12-11 Excelsior Wreath, made from packaging material.

Bring edges together at the back of the ring and fasten with a U-shaped stem piece. Continue around the ring, gathering Decorative Puff slightly as you go. Fasten every few inches with U stems. This should cover half the ring. Cover the other half with the other piece.

Make a bow with the white ribbon, fastening it at center with white chenille stem. Cut the stem to 3 inches and push into the ring. This will be the top of the wreath. Make a hanger in the back with 4 inches of green chenille stem. Glue a satin ball to the center of the bow.

The satin balls usually have stems. If not, add some. Use the stems to fasten the balls by pushing the stems into the wreath. Place a group of three satin balls on the wreath across from the bow. Then another group of three at quarter and three-quarter spaces around wreath. Now glue leaves under the balls.

· Excelsior Wreath ·

The wreath in Figure 12-11 is very inexpensive to make. Excelsior is the material that comes as packing for glassware and other breakables. If you don't have any, ask your favorite gift shop to save some for you. Straw can also be used.

MATERIALS

15″-diameter wire wreath frame
2 yd of 2¾″-wide (#40) red burlap
   ribbon
red chenille stem

10 medium-sized pine cones
excelsior
spool of #24 wire

INSTRUCTIONS

Take a handful of excelsior and wrap around the wire wreath frame. Then wrap #24 wire around the excelsior to hold it in place. Wrap the wire at an angle every 4 inches. Then add more excelsior and wire. Continue until the frame is covered. Twist the ends of the wire and hide ends in the excelsior.

Cut a 9-inch piece of wire, wrap around the wreath frame, and twist a loop at the back. This makes a hanger. We will call this point 12 o'clock.

Make a bow with the burlap ribbon. Tie very tightly at the center with the chenille stem. Lay the bow at the 3 o'clock position on the wreath and wrap the stem around to the back. Twist the stem to hold the bow in place.

Glue one pine cone on the bow center. Glue groupings of three pine cones at 6, 9, and 12 o'clock. Push the cones together tightly. Let the glue dry before hanging.

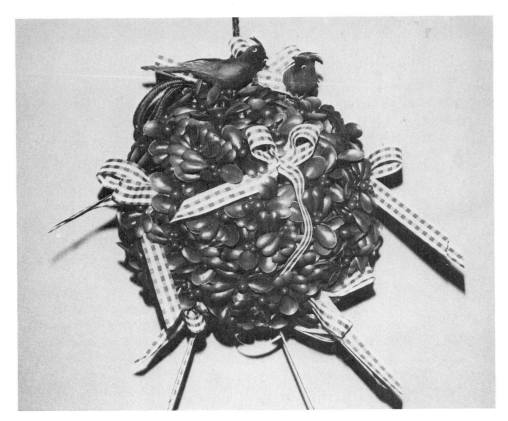

Fig. 12-12 Boxwood and Bows Hanging with redbirds.

· *Boxwood and Bows Hanging* ·

Figure 12-12 shows a quick idea to make a nice Noel hanging for the hallway.

MATERIALS

3″-diameter Styrofoam ball
two redbirds
3½ dozen artificial boxwood picks
6 yd of ⅝″-wide (#3) red and white
   gingham ribbon

1½ yd red velvet tubing
4 red chenille stems
2″ corsage pin
scissors
white glue

INSTRUCTIONS

Cut all the stems on the boxwood picks to 3-inch lengths. Push all the stems into the Styrofoam ball until it is completely covered.

    Make a bow with 24 inches of red velvet tubing. Fasten to the ball with glue and the corsage pin. This will be the top.

Make 12 bows, using 18-inch pieces of gingham ribbon. Tie each bow with a 4-inch piece of chenille stem. Then push the chenille stems into ball. Put a bow at top center and bottom center of ball. Then scatter the others around.

Fasten the redbirds to the top center of the ball, facing each other. Add the remaining tubing at the top of ball for hanging. Try this with other ribbon to fit your own color schemes.

· Patchwork Tree ·

The patchwork tree shown in color Figure 9, was fun, figuring which color ribbon to put at what spot. Leftover fabrics can be put to good use here.

MATERIALS

2 yd of ⁵⁄₁₆″-wide (#1½) red acetate ribbon

3 yd of ⅝″-wide (#3) red and white polka-dot ribbon

3 yd of 2¾″-wide (#40) ribbon, assorted colors

24″ flat-back Styrofoam tree
white glue
scissors
½″ brush
red chenille stem
clear acrylic spray glaze

INSTRUCTIONS

First, spread glue at bottom of the tree the width of the #40 ribbon. Then lay a strip of ribbon across from one side to the other side, pressing down as you go. Make sure any bubbles are smoothed out. Now do the same with another strip, butting it against the first. Repeat all the way to the top. Let it dry well, then trim away any excess ribbon at the edges. I prefer using the solid strips of ribbon to make sure the Styrofoam is completely covered.

Now glue the polka-dot ribbon around the side edges of the tree. While this dries, start cutting some hodge-podge pieces of ribbon. Use the scraps you have from trimming the edges, too.

Brush a small area of tree with glue and lay ribbon pieces at random in a crazy quilt motif. Be sure to leave some of the first glued ribbon exposed. Try overlapping some of the pieces—that adds dimension to your tree! You may need to cut a few pieces to fit some areas.

Attach the narrow red ribbon to the top edge with a thin line of glue, making a red border around the tree. Now brush a final coat of glue over the entire piece to smooth the surface. Then spray with three light coats of clear glaze. This acts as a protective coating.

Make a bow with the remaining polka-dot ribbon and glue it to the trunk of the tree.

Cut a 5-inch piece of chenille stem and attach it in back for a hanger, gluing the ends in place.

· Patchwork Candlestick ·

This project, shown in Figure 9 in the color section, complements the patchwork tree nicely. A pair of these would also make a delightful Christmas gift.

MATERIALS

8"-high wooden candlestick
1½ yd of 2¾"-wide (#40) ribbon,
    assorted colors
clear acrylic spray glaze
white glue

red acrylic paint
brush
#220 sandpaper
scissors
paper towel

INSTRUCTIONS

Sand the candlestick until it's smooth. Wipe away any dust with a damp towel.

Paint the wood with two coats of red, allowing about 30 minutes drying time between coats.

Cut the ribbons into small, odd shapes. Take a look at the finished project in the color section (Fig. 9) to see which areas I did not cover with ribbon: leave these borders show solid red.

Now spread glue on the candlestick in appropriate areas and press ribbon into place. Overlap some of your pieces. Make sure there are no red spaces showing between pieces. Remember to do the underneath edge. When all the ribbon is glued on, allow it to dry. Then spray three times with the glaze. This gives a hard protective coating.

· Li'l Miss ·

Pine cone boys and girls are fun to make. It's a good way to use up scraps of felt and ribbon, too. Make the one shown in color, Figure 9, then create some companions.

MATERIALS

2"-diameter Styrofoam ball
2 large green sequins
tiny red bead
18"of 2"-wide (#16) red Velvette
    ribbon
holly berry sprig
2½" x 2" pine cone for base

two 2" pine cones
two 1½" pine cones
36" of #24 wire
needle and thread
scissors
straight pins
white glue

Set the larger cone on its flat area. Put a piece of wire at the closed ends of the 2-inch cones and twist. Then join with the wire to the base of the larger cone. These are the legs. Repeat this procedure with the two small cones, then place them at top for the arms.

Push a piece of wire through the Styrofoam ball and attach it to the cone for a head.

Glue the sequins on for eyes and the bead for a nose. Cut a mouth from one corner of the ribbon and glue in place.

Cut 12 inches of ribbon. With needle and thread gather the ribbon at the edge. Push into the pine cone petals under the arms to make a skirt. Pull thread tight and glue in place.

Glue the holly sprig at center waist. Cut a piece of ribbon ¼ inch wide and 6 inches long, fold in center, and glue under the holly.

Cut a piece of ribbon 1 inch wide and 6 inches long and gather at one edge for hat. Pin in a circle and glue to top of her head. Cut another ribbon ¼ inch by 6 inches, fold in half, and pin on as trim for hat.

We sat our Li'l Miss in a doll's chair. How about at the edge of a centerpiece or atop a basket of crackers?

· *Creche* ·

The creche in Figure 12-13 was made with purchased nativity figurines, however, you could make and dress your own tiny characters.

Fig. 12-13 Miniature figurines in a seashell creche.

6″ of ⁵/₁₆″-wide (#1½) gold ribbon   2″ of #28 wire
miniature nativity set   sphagnum moss
large seashell   scissors
dried flowers   white glue

INSTRUCTIONS

Put a circle of glue in the back center of the shell and press the moss into it. Glue the nativity figures in position. Then glue small pieces of dried flowers in the back.

Make a bow and tie it with the wire. Cut off excess wire. Glue the bow at the top of the shell in the back.

13

JEWISH HOLIDAYS

· *Shalom* ·

These Jewish symbols come in Styrofoam, ready to trim and use. The Shalom is shown in Figure 13-1.

MATERIALS

blue Styrofoam shalom
3 gold leaves
1¼ yd ⅝"-wide (#3) royal blue
   Velvette ribbon
royal blue chenille stem

3 yd gold braid
2 gold paper seals
scissors
white glue

INSTRUCTIONS

Glue the royal Velvette ribbon around the side edge of the base. Then glue the gold braid around the top edge of the base and along the center of each letter (Fig. 13-1). Be sure to cut the braid at the end of each letter.

    Under the letter S, glue the three gold leaves. Make a single bow from the royal blue ribbon and tie with a short piece of chenille stem. Push stem into Styrofoam in the center of the leaves.

    Glue the two gold seals under the O and M.

· *Golden Menorah* ·

This traditional Hebrew candelabrum is used at Hanukkah.

MATERIALS

1½ yd ⅝"-wide (#3) royal blue
   Velvette ribbon
Styrofoam menorah
gold glitter
royal blue chenille stem

thin white glue
½" brush
scissors
waxed paper
box lid

Fig. 13-1 Shalom, Golden Menorah, and Dreidels for the Jewish holidays.

INSTRUCTIONS

Brush thin glue on one side and along the edges of each section of the Styrofoam. Sprinkle the gold glitter into the glue. Remember to work over a box lid so you can save the extra glitter. Set aside on waxed paper to dry.

Make a bow with the blue ribbon and tie at center with a 3-inch piece of chenille stem. Push the end of the stem into the Styrofoam below the candle sections, as shown in Figure 13-1.

· *Dreidels* ·

Traditional dreidels are four-sided dies that spin like tops. They are used as toys, especially during the Hanukkah season.

MATERIALS

two 4″ x 7″ Styrofoam dreidels
1 yd of 1″-wide red eyelash trim
14″ of 1″ wide red and gold braid
14″ small red metallic braid
1 yd gold braid
1 package gold paper trims
1 yd small blue braid

5″ of $1^7/_{16}$″-wide (#9) royal
   Velvette ribbon
5″ of $1^7/_{16}$″-wide (#9) white
   Velvette ribbon
scissors
white glue

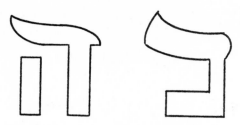

Fig. 13-2 Hebrew letter patterns for the dreidels.

INSTRUCTIONS

These dreidels come in two pieces which interlock for easy assembling. First we'll decorate the piece with the handle. Glue the gold braid on both sides of the outside edge. Then glue the tiny blue braid to the edges of the large flat section. Cut letters from blue and white ribbon. In the center of each side of this flat part, glue a Hebrew letter (Fig. 13-2). Then, on either side of this, glue a gold paper trim.

Now glue the wide red and gold braid along the edge of the insert piece.

Trim the other dreidel in the same manner, using the wide red braid where you used the small gold on the first.

14

GRADUATION

· Graduate's Gift ·

I made this gift box in Figure 14-1 for our son, Jim, who graduated from high school this year.

MATERIALS

4½" x 6" unfinished wooden box
graduation announcement and
    name card
gold braid
½" brush
walnut stain
white glue

#220 sandpaper
#400 sandpaper
clear acrylic spray glaze
lintfree cloth
scissors
plastic bag

INSTRUCTIONS

Sand the box and lid with #220 sandpaper until they are very smooth. Wipe the dust away with a lintfree cloth. Brush on the stain and wipe off excess. If the box is not as dark as you'd like it, brush on more stain. The stain brings up the nap of the wood and we need a smooth surface to work with, so sand again with #400 sandpaper after it dries.

The announcement I used was the exact size of the lid. If the one you're using isn't, cut it to fit. Spread thin white glue with your fingers over the entire lid. Lay the announcement at the top of the box and slowly press into place. If you don't get it on straight, reposition it quickly before the glue dries. To make sure all extra glue and air bubbles are removed, lay a plastic bag over the announcement and press with your fingers from the center toward the edges. Wipe away the extra glue with a damp paper towel.

Glue the name card at the center end of the box as shown (Fig. 14-1). Then glue the gold braid around the announcement and name card. Let dry overnight.

The next day, spray the entire surface of the box with the clear glaze. If this is to be a jewelry box, line it with felt or velvet. If the box is to serve another purpose, stain and glaze the inside of the box.

Fig. 14-1 Graduate's Gift box with keepsake announcement.

· Framed Announcement ·

Our daughter Sue's college graduation announcement was used for the idea shown in Figure 14-2. When our other four children graduate from college we'll have quite a collection.

MATERIALS

announcement
wooden frame, same size as
   announcement
glass pane to fit frame
gold leaf base paint
gold leaf adhesive
gold leaf sheets

gold leaf sealer
mat board
#220 sandpaper
paper towel
soft brush
scissors
white glue

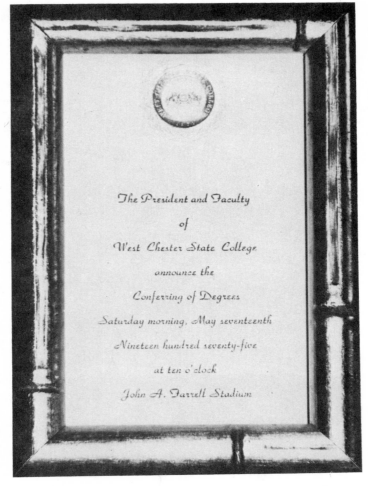

Fig. 14-2 Framed graduation announcement.

INSTRUCTIONS

Sand the frame smooth with #220 sandpaper. Apply one coat of the gold leaf base paint. Let this dry for one hour. Repeat the sanding and painting a second time.

When this is dry, spray with gold leaf adhesive and let it dry about 30 minutes. It should be tacky.

Slide the gold leaf sheets onto the frame and brush over them very carefully with a soft brush to make them stick to the frame. Overlap each sheet between ⅛ and ¼ inch. Cover the entire frame in this manner. Let this dry overnight, then seal with gold leaf sealer. Now let the frame dry for one week before handling.

Cut a piece of mat board to fit the frame. Trim the part of the announcement you'll be using. Glue this to the mat board. Set aside to dry.

Have a piece of glass cut to fit the inside lip of the frame. Glue the glass in place.

Now glue the announcement and the mat board to the back of the frame.

· *Graduate* ·

The figurine (Fig. 14-3) would make a nice surprise for your graduate, or use it as a centerpiece for the celebration dinner.

MATERIALS

half of a 2″-diameter Styrofoam ball
1″-diameter Styrofoam ball
12″-high Styrofoam cone
3″-diameter satin ball
1 package black Decorative Puff
16″ of 2″-wide (#9) white ribbon
4″ of 2¾″-wide (#16) gold velvette ribbon
9″ x 12″ black felt
2 white jumbo chenille stems

3″ gold tassel
6mm red bead
two 15mm wiggle eyes
pearl head corsage pin
black spray paint
4″ x 4″ poster board
18 straight pins
6″ of #28 wire
scissors
white glue

INSTRUCTIONS

Spray the 12-inch cone with black paint. Let dry. To make the graduate's cap, glue the 4-inch square of poster board onto one corner of the black felt. Cut out the square. Glue the other side of the poster board to the felt and cut out again.

Lay the rounded part of the half Styrofoam ball in the center of the felt. Cut a piece of felt large enough to cover the ball. Spread glue on the ball and stretch the felt over the rounded part of the ball. Be careful to smooth out all wrinkles and folds. Trim away excess felt. After this is dry, glue a piece of felt to the flat part of the ball and trim. Glue the 4-inch felt square to the rounded part of the ball, pushing together to flatten the ball slightly. Let the cap dry.

The holes in the satin ball will be the top and bottom. Cut two eye-shaped pieces from black felt each about 1 inch long. Glue one wiggle eye onto each felt piece. Glue the eyes in position on the satin ball. Glue and pin the red bead in position for a nose.

While this dries, we'll dress the graduate. Pull the Decorative Puff apart so you have half the thickness. With a razor or scissors, cut a piece of black Decorative Puff 12 inches by 18 inches. Spread glue around the top of the cone. Lay one corner of the 18-inch edge of Decorative Puff into the glue and gather and pin the gown as you drape the Decorative Puff around the cone. Overlap the seam about ½ inch.

Fig. 14-3 Graduate in cap and gown.

This seam will be in the back. Cut a 6-inch piece of #28 wire and tie tightly around the gathers in the gown. Twist the wire together at the back and cut away the excess.

We'll make the sleeves now. Cut two pieces of Decorative Puff, each 4 inches by 6 inches. Cut each jumbo chenille stem so that you have two 7-inch pieces. Lay one stem on a sleeve piece lengthwise, with ½ inch of stem extending beyond each end. Spread glue on the stem and roll the Decorative Puff around it, into a tube shape. Hold for a few seconds until the glue sets. Repeat for the other sleeve. Push one end of each arm into the cone at the top, pin and glue. Remember to have the arms coming from the back. They should be pushed into the Styrofoam about ¾ inch apart. Bend around to the front, shaping the arms, and bend a little at the elbows.

Cut the 1-inch Styrofoam ball in half. Now cut a small wedge shape from each piece to form thumbs. Be sure to do the cuts opposite, so you have a right and left hand. Squeeze the Styrofoam at the wrist position to make it smaller than the hand. Put glue on the end of each chenille stem and push into the wrist, keeping the thumbs up.

Put a 1-inch by 6-inch piece of Decorative Puff around the neckline and glue in place. This will hide the wires.

Cut the white ribbon in half. Lay each piece across the shoulders, as shown in Figure 14-3. Glue the ribbon together where it crosses. Then cut it into pointed ends, front and back. Now glue the ribbon to the robe.

Fold the gold ribbon in half for a diploma. Glue a short piece of black felt inside on the fold. Now glue diploma in the graduate's hand.

The hat and head should be dry now. Position the hat on the head and press together to make a good fit. Then spread glue between them and join by pushing corsage pin through end of the tassel and down through the hat and head.

Cut a 1½-inch piece of chenille stem and glue into hole in the bottom of the satin ball. Then put glue on the top of the cone and push the stem into the cone. Make sure it's in all the way.

This is a good money-making project. Make graduates in your school's colors and sell them to your friends.

· *Graduation Panorama* ·

This idea, shown in Figure 14-4, makes a cute little favor or a nice remembrance gift.

MATERIALS

32″ gold gimp
18″ of 2″-wide (#16) gold Velvette
 ribbon
15″ of 2″-wide (#16) blue Velvette
 ribbon
large tuna or similar-sized can

2 graduate miniatures
1″ x 3½″ Styrofoam block, ¼″ thick
3″ gold tassel
1½″ plastic curtain ring
white glue

INSTRUCTIONS

Cut both ends off the tuna can. Wash thoroughly. Press the can into an oval shape, with the seam on one of the flat sides.

Measure ribbon for length around the can. Also make sure it fits

Fig. 14-4 Graduation Panorama with tiny figurines.

inside the rim. Spread glue on the outside of the can, except the rim. Keep ribbon seam at can seam. This will be the bottom. Lay the blue ribbon in glue and press out any bubbles or wrinkles. Now glue the gold ribbon to the inside in the same way. Glue a half width of the gimp to the inside of the rim, and then fold to the outside and glue. This will cover the entire rim. Do both rims.

Cut two pieces of gold velvette ribbon, 1½ inches square. Roll each to resemble a diploma and tie with a small piece of blue ribbon. Glue to the top of the can. Glue the plastic ring to the bottom of the can to form a stand. Set aside to dry.

Cut one piece of Styrofoam ¼ by 1 by 2 inches and another ¼ by 1 by 1½ inches. Cover the large piece with blue ribbon and the small piece with gold ribbon to resemble books. Glue the two books to the center of the can. Then glue a miniature graduate to each side. Glue the tassel on at center back so it hangs down behind the books.

BRIDAL SHOWER

· Invitation ·

This watering can with silver and pink flowers makes a delightful adornment for the shower invitation (Fig. 15-1).

MATERIALS

5½″ x 6½″ white stationery
4″ of 2¾″-wide (#40) pink satin
  ribbon
6 green sequin leaves
6 large silver sequins

6 small pink sequins
pencil
green felt-tip pen, fine point
scissors
white glue

INSTRUCTIONS

Fold the stationery in half so that the invitation will measure 3¼ inches by 5½ inches. Using the pattern in Figure 15-2, trace on the wrong side of the ribbon with a pencil. Cut out the can. Glue to the bottom of the invitation at an angle.

Fig. 15-1 Decorations for a bridal shower: basket, sprinkling can favor, invitation, matchbook, and parasol.

Fig. 15-2 Sprinkling can pattern for invitation.

Glue five large sequins as flowers around the top opening of the can. Glue the pink sequins as flower centers, then add the leaf sequins around the flowers. This makes a nice bouquet.

Glue one flower and leaf to the upper lefthand corner of the invitation.

Outline the watering can with the green felt-tip pen. Also write "Bridal Shower" above the watering can then add the details about the party inside.

· *Sweetheart Centerpiece* ·

This is such a lovely creation that you might like to vary the colors and theme for other occasions; the completed project is shown in color (Fig. 10).

MATERIALS

10″ x 12″ Styrofoam cutout heart, 1½″ thick
half of a 3″-diameter Styrofoam ball
6″-diameter Styrofoam disc, 1″ thick
3 yd pink marvel lace
2½ yd white velvet tubing

2½ yd string pink beads
two 5-inch white doves
toothpicks
pencil
white glue
scissors
straight pins

INSTRUCTIONS

First, decorate the heart shape. Cut a 2-yard length of lace. Starting at the point at the bottom of the Styrofoam heart, spread glue on the top side of the heart for just a few inches. As you lay the lace in the glue, make small gathers and pin the gathers to the Styrofoam. Continue in this manner to cover the entire heart. Do not hurry—take your time. Let this dry thoroughly.

Cut a 1-yard length of velvet tubing and 1½ yards of pink beads. At the point of the heart, glue one end of both the tubing and string of beads to the center of the lace and secure with a straight pin. As you continue around the heart shape, wrap the beads around the tubing and glue in place. The beads should wrap once around the tubing about every inch, candystick style. Secure with straight pins as you go. Be careful not to smear the glue.

Using half a yard of tubing, make a bow and tie it with 10 inches of the pink beads. Glue and pin the bow at the top of the heart.

With the flat surface of the half ball on the table, glue the center of the disc on top of the hemisphere and secure with toothpicks.

Fold the remaining lace in half lengthwise. Glue the fold of the lace around the side of the disc, gathering and pinning as you did for the heart. Let this dry. Then, wrap the string of beads around the velvet tubing as before and glue this around the disc over the lace at fold edge. Secure with pins and let dry. When all the glue has dried, remove the pins.

Put four toothpicks and glue in the point of the heart and push into the disc. The heart should be slightly off center. Secure the doves in front of the heart. Put in the center of your party table with the pretty pink parasol in the next project and you're ready for guests.

· Pink Parasol ·

We're very excited about out parasol centerpiece, shown in color in Figure 10. The chenille is very sparkling and the lace gives the parasol an airy feeling. When the shower is over, pack the centerpiece away in a plastic bag and keep it fresh for another time.

MATERIALS

15″ open parasol wire frame	scissors
3 yd pink marvel lace	white glue
1 hank pink 2″-bump chenille	

INSTRUCTIONS

Cut the chenille into 3-yard pieces. This makes it so much easier to work with. Start at the end of spokes and wrap the chenille around very tightly just at the end. Continue wrapping around and around close together so as to cover the wire. Do all wire sections this way. Then starting at the top, wrap the handle. Be sure that you wrap all cut ends tightly. Set this aside for now.

It will take two rows of lace around the parasol. And each section is determined by the spokes. So we have six sections, each with two pieces.

Cut a piece of lace 9½ inches long at the base and taper to the top at 6½ inches. Lay on the frame at the bottom of a section, extending about 1¼ inches over the outside edge. It should overlap the side wires. When you're sure it is a perfect fit, cut five more pieces the same. Glue one piece on the frame, remembering to extend the lace 1¼ inches over bottom of frame. Press the chenille and lace together.

Cut a piece of lace 6 inches long at the base and taper to the top 1½ inches. Lay this piece overlapping the glued piece about ¼ inch—just enough so the other side touches the top center of the parasol. Cut five more pieces of lace the same.

Glue the larger lace pieces all around the frame in the six sections. Let dry for one hour, then trim off any excess. Then glue the other pieces around the top. Make sure all pieces are secure at top center.

Put this aside to dry for about an hour. Then trim away the excess lace.

Place the wrapped gifts under the pretty pink parasol.

· Shower Favors ·

Make one or several of these little party favors shown in Figure 15-1 for each guest.

· PARASOL FAVOR ·

MATERIALS

half of a 3″-diameter Styrofoam ball	diamond dust
white chenille stem	white glue
24″ string pink beads	small brush
½″ x 24″ silver braid	scissors
	pencil

INSTRUCTIONS

With a pencil, draw a line dividing the curved surface of the ball in half and then in half again. Spread glue on the lines and press the braid into it. Glue the braid around the bottom edge. Make sure it's pressed in place. Now put a thin line of glue down the center of the braid and attach the pink beads. The beads will cross over each other at center top.

While this dries, cut a 5-inch piece of chenille stem. Make a hook in one end for the parasol handle. Starting at the hook, glue the beads on the handle, leaving ¼ inch of stem end plain. Put a dab of glue on this end of stem and push into the center of flat side of the ball. Let dry.

With the small brush, spread glue over the entire ball, including the trims. Sprinkle with diamond dust. Let dry for an hour.

Make a bow with remainder of the braid and tie in center with short piece of stem. Glue to center top of the parasol.

· BRIDAL BASKET FAVOR ·

MATERIALS

half of a 3″-diameter Styrofoam ball
12″ of ½″-wide gold and white lace
17″ green velvet tubing
5″ x 10″ white net
white chenille stem

diamond dust
pearl stand, daisy shaped
bunch of white lilies of the valley
scissors
white glue

INSTRUCTIONS

Spread glue over the curved section of the half Styrofoam ball and sprinkle diamond dust over it. Set aside to dry for about half an hour.

Cut an 8-inch length of tubing and push the chenille stem through it, leaving ½ inch of stem stick out of each end. This will be the handle, so set it aside for now.

Cut a piece of lace long enough to go around the cut edge of the ball and glue it in place. Make sure the ends meet and are glued down. Now cut a length of tubing and glue it over the edge of the lace. Glue the pearl stand onto the center of the curved surface of the Styrofoam. Position the basket handle on the flat surface and push each end into the Styrofoam.

Cut the net into two 5 by 5 inch pieces. Gather through the center and secure with a 3-inch length of chenille stem. Then push one piece of net into the Styrofoam on each side of the handle. Glue three flowers at each end of handle on Styrofoam.

Save one stem of flowers for later. Arrange the rest of the flowers on both sides of the handle.

Gather the edge of the remaining lace and make into a fan shape. Glue to the top center of the handle. Glue three tiny flowers in the center of the lace.

· DECORATED MATCHBOOK ·

MATERIALS

1½″ x 4½″ pink satin polka-dot ribbon
2 miniature white leaves
3 miniature white flowers

matchbook
6 hair clips
scissors
white glue

Unfold the matchbook and spread glue on outside surface, except for the striking surface. Lay the ribbon into the glue and smooth out with your fingers. Put the hair clips along the edges until the glue dries. Clean up any excess glue with a damp paper towel.

When dry, fold the matchbook back to its original shape. Cut the stems from the leaves and the flowers. Glue the flowers and stems to the center of the matchbook.

Now make several for favors at your shower. Vary the colors if you'd like.

· SPRINKLING CAN FAVOR ·

There are many small plastic favors on the market today. All can be decorated and trimmed in various ways. This is just one suggestion for you, shown in Figure 15-1.

MATERIALS

1½"-high pink plastic sprinkling can
8" silver braid
small pink flowers

⅛" x 6" velvet ribbon
scissors
white glue

INSTRUCTIONS

Glue silver braid around the top and bottom edges of the can. Make a bow from the velvet ribbon and glue to the handle.

Cut the stems of the flowers to the depth of the little can and glue them into place. Try this in different colors.

16

WEDDING

· *Bride and Bridegroom* ·

What better way to make the most special occasion even more memorable than with lovingly handmade decorations? The Bride and Bridegroom centerpiece is shown in the color section, Figure 11.

MATERIALS

two 5″ x 4″ Styrofoam pedestals, 4″ high
30″ stem wire
1 yd white velvet tubing
1½ yd ½″-wide silver braid
3 bunches white cloth lilies of the valley
3½″-high bride and bridegroom set

3 sprigs white cloth leaves
2 white chenille stems
diamond dust
white floral tape
wire cutters
white glue
scissors
spray adhesive

INSTRUCTIONS

Cut the larger dome off one of the Styrofoam pedestals. Save the pedestal for another project; you only need the larger dome for this arrangement. Apply spray adhesive to all surfaces of the uncut pedestal and the large dome, except the flat surface of the small dome on the pedestal. Sprinkle diamond dust onto these surfaces. Let this dry overnight.

Glue silver braid around the edges of all three domes.

Gather three stems of lilies and three stems of leaves, twisting the stems together. Put glue on the ends of the stems and push into the leg of the pedestal near the small dome, which is the base. This will be the front of the pedestal.

Cut the chenille stems into 3-inch lengths. Gather three lilies and twist a piece of chenille stem around the stems of the lilies. Wrap the twist in white floral tape. Follow these directions, using the leaves, lilies, chenille, and floral tape to make five more bunches: one with five stems of lilies, two with three stems of leaves, one with four stems of lilies, and one with three stems of lilies. Arrange these six bunches in fan fashion and push the stems into the Styrofoam one inch behind the center on the flat top of the pedestal.

Glue the bride and bridegroom in front of the fan of flowers and leaves.

Cut the wire into six 5-inch lengths. Cover each wire with 4 inches of white velvet tubing, leaving ½ inch of the wire uncovered at each end. Insert two wires into the pedestal at each side of the bride and groom and two behind the floral fan, to serve as columns.

Place the flat surface of the top dome over the wires. When you have the dome *centered* over the pedestal, push the dome into the wires to secure its position. Be sure the wires are straight.

Arrange two stems of lilies and six stems of leaves in a circle around the center of the top dome. Push the stems into the Styrofoam. The stems in front should lie flat against the dome and the stems in the back should be slightly elevated.

Make a double-loop bow from the remaining tubing and secure with a length of chenille stem. Insert the stem into the center of the floral arrangement on top of the dome.

· *Wedding Bells* ·

The wicker bells shown in color, Figure 11, are a perfect complement to the Bride and Groom centerpiece. The materials and instructions are for one wedding bell.

MATERIALS

7″-high wicker bell
1¹⁄₆ yd of 1⁷⁄₁₆″-wide (#9) white iridescent ribbon
1¹⁄₆ yd of ⅜″-wide silver flat braid
2 white chenille stems
five 4″ stems of white cloth lilies of the valley

miniature plastic dove
1¼″-diameter white satin ball
white spray paint
diamond dust
spray adhesive
scissors
white glue

INSTRUCTIONS

Spray the inside and outside of the bell with white paint. Let the paint dry thoroughly. Then spray adhesive over the entire outside surface of the bell. Sprinkle diamond dust onto the adhesive while it is still wet. Allow to dry.

Glue the silver braid along the center of the white ribbon. Cut a point in each end of the ribbon. When the glue has dried, make a double bow and secure the center with an 8-inch piece of chenille stem.

Twist the ends of the flower stems together. Glue the bunch of flowers at the top of the bell, with the flowers laying down at the front. Place the bow on top of the flowers and twist the stem around the ring on top of the bell. Set the dove in the middle of the bow and fasten in place with glue.

Fasten a chenille stem to the top inside of the bell, and cut the stem even with the bottom of the bell. Now fasten the satin ball to the stem for the bell clapper.

· Reception Favors ·

Guests always like to have a small keepsake from the wedding. Four ideas are shown in Figure 12, color section, and instructions follow. You might try making one or several of these favors for each guest to keep.

· MATCHBOOK ·

MATERIALS

4½″ of 1⁷⁄₁₆″-wide (#9) white
    iridescent ribbon
8″ silver double-loop braid
3 white cloth lilies of the valley

matchbook
2 miniature white bells
scissors
white glue

INSTRUCTIONS

Open the matchbook and glue the ribbon onto the cover. Be sure not to cover the striking surface of the matchbook.

Glue silver braid along the two longer edges of the matchbook. Decorate the front by gluing the lilies and bells in place.

· PLACE CARD ·

MATERIALS

4″ x 4½″ white poster board
1 stem white cloth lilies of the
    valley
2 silver-colored plastic wedding
    bands

13″ silver double-loop braid
black felt-tip pen
scissors
white glue

INSTRUCTIONS

Fold the poster board in half so it measures 2 inches by 4½ inches. Glue silver braid around one half of the poster board: this will be the front of the place card.

Curl the stem of flowers around your finger and glue the flowers to the left on the front. Glue the wedding bands upright in the center of the lilies. Write the guest's name on the card with a felt-tip pen.

· BELL FAVOR ·

MATERIALS

2½"-high white plastic bell
6" x 6" white net
5 stems of white cloth lilies of the
   valley

10" of ⅜"-wide (#1½) white velvet
   ribbon
2 silver-colored wedding bands
5" of #28 wire

INSTRUCTIONS

Sit the bell in the center of the net. Bring the net up around the bell and gather at the top, securing the gathers by twisting the #28 wire around the net.

Glue the stems of the lilies at the top of the bell; have all stems meeting at a common point and the flowers extending downward.

Tie the ribbon around the bell to cover the wire and make a bow. Glue the rings to the knot in the bow.

· EGG FAVOR ·

MATERIALS

open-sided plastic egg on stand
1"-high bride and bridegroom
   figurines
12" of ⁵⁄₁₆"-wide (#1½) white
   velvet ribbon

13" string 3mm pearls
12mm pearl crown
silver glitter
scissors
white glue

INSTRUCTIONS

Spread glue over the entire plastic egg and stand, inside and out. Sprinkle glitter into the glue. Let this dry.

Glue ribbon around the biggest part of the egg, starting at the stand. Glue a string of pearls onto the center of the ribbon. Glue pearls around the base of the egg stand.

Make a bow from the velvet ribbon and glue onto the stand.

Inside the egg, glue the pearl crown on the bottom. Glue the bride and bridegroom into position on the crown.

· Book Invitation ·

I used an invitation from our John and Maureen's wedding for this idea, which has become a family treasure (Fig. 12, color section).

MATERIALS

8″ x 12″ Styrofoam open book
    shape, 1″ thick
12″ of ⅜″-wide flat silver braid
22″ silver double-loop braid
appropriate print
wedding invitation

craft stick
diamond dust
silver glitter
white glue
scissors
spray adhesive

INSTRUCTIONS

Cut the excess border from the print you have chosen and glue to the lefthand page of the book. Trim the invitation to measure 4 by 6½ inches. Center the invitation on the righthand page of the book and make a small mark on the Styrofoam at one of its corners. Then spread glue evenly on the back of the invitation and position it on the book. Starting at the center of the invitation, press it firmly but gently to the book, smoothing it out toward the edges. This releases air bubbles and excess glue.

Glue the silver loop braid along the edges of the invitation. Do not cut the braid at each corner; instead, ease the braid into a rounded corner. Let this dry overnight.

Apply a coat of spray adhesive to the surface of the book, print, and invitation. Sprinkle silver glitter on the page edges. Sprinkle diamond dust on the rest of the book, print, and invitation. Before the adhesive dries completely, use the craft stick to remove the diamond dust from the names of the bride and bridegroom.

Cut a point in each end of the flat silver braid and lay in the center of the open book as a bookmark.

17

BABY SHOWER

· *Bonnet Invitation* ·

The color scheme of the invitation shown in Figure 13, color section, and Figure 17-1—as well as the other party decorations—can be varied to suit the occasion.

MATERIALS

5″ x 7″ pink stationery
24″ of ⁵/₁₆″-wide (#1½) pink satin
   ribbon
8″ of ½″-wide gold lace

5″ x 7″ pink marvel lace
scissors
white glue

INSTRUCTIONS

Following the pattern outline in Figure 17-2, cut a bonnet shape from the stationery and the marvel lace. Run a thin line of glue around the edge of the paper and press the marvel lace into the glue. Fold the

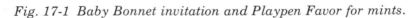

Fig. 17-1 Baby Bonnet invitation and Playpen Favor for mints.

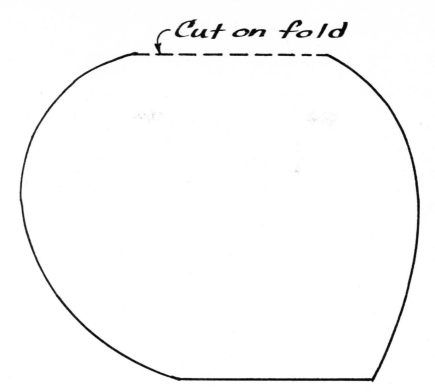

Fig. 17-2 Pattern for bonnet invitation.

invitation and proceed to decorate the front. While the glue is still wet, trim the edge on the front of the invitation with the pink satin ribbon.

Glue the gold lace along the back bottom of the invitation, around the folded edge, and across the front (Fig. 17-1). Make a bow from the pink ribbon and glue at the end of the lace in front. Complete the invitation by writing the details of the party on the inside page.

· *Playpen Favor* ·

Your guests will be delighted to keep the shower favor shown in Figure 17-1 and in color (Fig. 13).

MATERIALS

2″ x 2″ Styrofoam block, ½″ thick
16 toothpicks .
24″ of ⁵/₁₆″-wide (#1½) blue satin
  ribbon
2″ x 3″ pink gingham

1 small blue flower
1 miniature baby doll
scissors
white glue

Trim the gingham to fit one side of the Styrofoam block, then glue it onto the Styrofoam. Place a dab of glue on one end of each toothpick and push the glued end into the Styrofoam. Space the toothpicks evenly along each edge of the Styrofoam (Fig. 17-1). There will be a toothpick at each corner of the block and three between each corner.

Cut the blue ribbon into three 8-inch lengths. Glue one strip around the bottom edge of the Styrofoam. Glue a strip around the outside tops of the toothpicks, and another inside the tops, to form a railing. Cut the remaining gingham into ½-inch strips and make a bow. Glue the bow to the ribbon railing and fasten the flower to the middle of the bow. Fill the playpen with candy mints and set the baby doll on the mints.

· *Baby's Gift Box* ·

Make a very special box for the new arrival—a lasting gift his parents will use to save his first booties and other tiny memories. The finished box is shown in Figure 17-3 and in the color section, Figure 13.

Fig. 17-3 Stork and Baby's Gift Box.

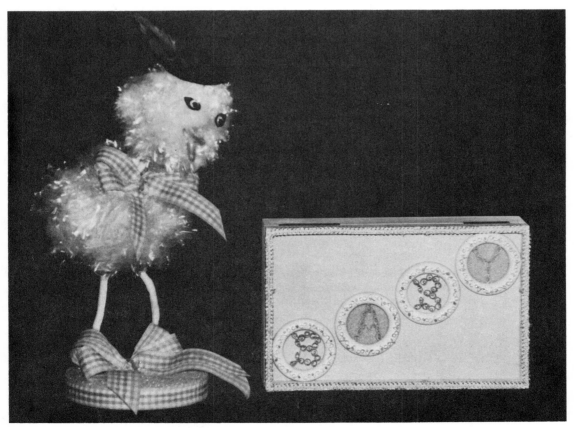

MATERIALS

four 1¾″-diameter wooden rings
6 strips pink quilling paper
8 strips baby blue quilling paper
1 yd pink and blue double-loop
   braid
#233 Heirloom wood box
glass pane to fit inverted box lid
15″ x 25″ baby blue felt
gesso
white acrylic paint
pink acrylic paint
paint brush
#220 sandpaper

#400 sandpaper
hinges
clasp fastener
screwdriver
scissors
ruler
tracing paper
pencil
round toothpick
paper bag
clear acrylic spray glaze
silicone adhesive
white glue

INSTRUCTIONS

Sand the outside of the box with #220 sandpaper to a smooth finish. Pay special attention to the corners. Clean the sawdust off the box. Be sure the paint brush is clean and paint two coats of Gesso over the entire box. When the Gesso has dried, sand with the #400 sandpaper. Paint the outside of the box with two coats of pink. The paint may raise the nap in the wood; if so, sand very carefully with #400 sandpaper and paint again. The lid will be inverted for a shadow-box effect, so paint the inside and edges of the lid also. Paint the wooden rings white. After all the paint dries, spray all wood pieces with three light coats of spray glaze.

The letters in the word BABY are formed using a variety of quilling shapes. I have selected vee, eye, tight roll, and loose roll shapes. Tight rolls are formed by gluing the loose end of the quilling paper while the shape remains on the toothpick. Loose rolls are formed by gluing the loose end after removing the paper from the toothpick and allowing it to stretch to its natural shape. Practice making the rolls until you have uniform sizes and shapes.

Using the pink quilling paper, tear forty-nine 1¼-inch-long strips and sixteen 2½-inch-long strips. Make twenty-four tight rolls from the 1¼-inch strips. To roll the paper, place the end of the paper on your first finger and hold with the end of the toothpick as shown in Figure 17-4. Now pinch the paper and toothpick lightly between your thumb and finger, then twist the toothpick, rolling the strip onto the toothpick. The beginning of the roll should be tightly wound. Then relax your hold on the roll and continue rolling the strip to the end. Glue the loose end to the roll.

Make sixteen loose rolls from the 2½-inch pink strips. Loose rolls are started following the same procedure as tight rolls. When the strip is completely rolled onto the toothpick, do not glue the end. Slide the roll off of the toothpick and lay it on the table. The roll will loosen to its somewhat larger shape. Then glue the loose end to the roll.

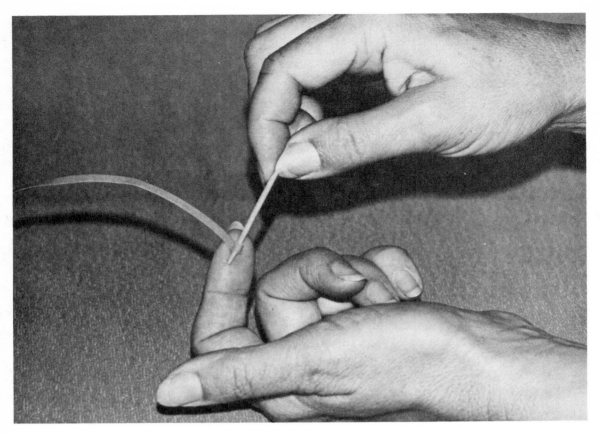

Fig. 17-4 Positioning toothpick and paper to begin quilling.

Shape six loose rolls into raindrops by pinching a circle at the point where the loose end was glued, as shown in Figure 17-5.

Form nine loose rolls into eye shapes by gently pinching the circle twice, leaving the filigree round in the center.

Form one heart shape by holding the roll between your thumb and forefinger. Use your other forefinger to dent in the center of the circle and press the sides together.

Make twenty-five vee shapes, using 1¼-inch-long pink strips. Fold a strip in half, then roll each end toward the center on the article. Slide the roll off the toothpick and let it expand to its natural shape. Do not glue the ends.

From the blue quilling paper cut two 2-inch strips, tear forty-eight 1¼-inch strips, and thirty 2½-inch strips. Make twenty-four tight rolls and twenty-four vee shapes from the 1¼-inch strips. Make thirty loose rolls from the 2½-inch strips. Form four loose rolls into eye shapes and four loose rolls into raindrops.

Trace the letters *B, A, B, Y,* 1½ inches high, onto white paper, following the pattern in Figure 17-6. Lay waxed paper over the lettering and form the letters by gluing the quilled pieces together. Use the loose

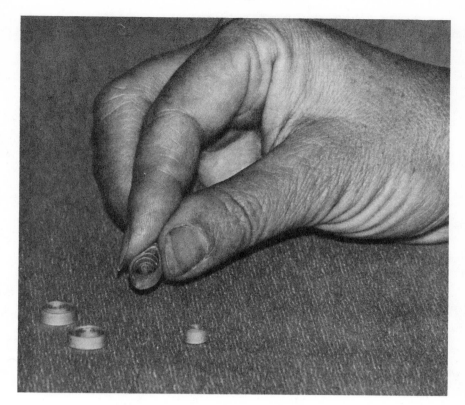

Fig. 17-5 Completed quilling shapes.

blue shapes for the *Bs.* Form the stroke of the *B* first by gluing two eye shapes and two raindrops to an unrolled 2-inch blue strip. Then form the loops of the *B* by gluing loose rolls together. Use the loose pink shapes for the *A* and *Y.* The eye shapes are used to form each stroke of the letters, with raindrops placed at the end of each stroke. A pink vee is used for the crossbar on the *A,* and the heart shape is used in the center of the *Y.*

Cut two 2½-inch circles from the blue felt and glue as backing on two of the wooden rings. Now glue the *A* and the *Y* into the center of

Fig. 17-6   Pattern for lettering Baby's Gift Box.

these wooden rings. The *Bs* are held in the center of the other two rings by gluing the quilled paper where it touches the inside edges of the rings. Glue twelve blue vees around the front of each of the *A* and *Y* rings. Alternate the direction in which the point in the vee is positioned. Next, glue a pink tight roll inside each vee. Glue twelve pink vees on each of the *B* rings and glue blue tight rolls inside each vee.

With the box lid inverted, glue the letter rings to the inside of the lid so that the word *BABY* rises from bottom left to top right corner. Spread a thin line of silicone adhesive on the edge of the lid and press the pane of glass into the adhesive. Trim the edge of the glass by gluing the pink and blue loop braid in place.

The inside of the box is lined, using the blue felt. Each side, the bottom, and the top should be covered with separate pieces of felt. Make a pattern for each piece, using the paper bag. The pattern for the inside top piece should be cut smaller than the lid to allow for thickness of box sides. Thus the lid will fit flush when closed.

Following your pattern, cut each piece from the blue felt. Glue the side pieces in place first. Next glue the bottom piece in place, and finally glue the lid piece in position, remembering to leave a margin around the edges. Set aside to dry.

To complete the gift box, attach the hinges and clasp.

· *Stork* ·

Now it's time to make the guest of honor—our friend shown in the color section, Figure 13, and in Figure 17-3.

MATERIALS

2″-diameter Styrofoam ball
4″ Styrofoam egg
75 Baggies, sandwich size
19 white chenille stems
20″ white velvet tubing
2 pink chenille stems
8 pink jumbo chenille stems
6″ x 6″ black felt
two 10mm wiggle eyes
3″ x 3″ poster board
1¼″-diameter Styrofoam ball

pink feather
2½ yd of 1⁷/₁₆″-wide (#9) pink
    gingham ribbon
2½ yd of ⅝″-wide (#3) blue
    gingham ribbon
6″-diameter Styrofoam disc
10″-diameter Styrofoam disc
coat hanger
heavy wire cutters
scissors
white glue

INSTRUCTIONS

The stork's head and body are made by covering the 2-inch ball and the 4-inch egg with plastic puffs made from sandwich bags. First, cut the chenille stems into 3-inch lengths. Then cut the sealed ends off all the plastic sandwich bags.

See Figures 7-6 through 7-8 and accompanying instructions under *Bonnet Centerpiece,* Ch. 7, for step by step directions on making plastic puffs. Make seventy-five puffs, then come back to this project for the next procedure.

Cover both Styrofoam pieces with the puffs by pushing the chenille stems into the Styrofoam. The ball for the stork's head will take thirty puffs and the egg-shaped body will require forty-five puffs.

Cut the coat hanger into two 10-inch lengths and two 4-inch lengths. Cut the velvet tubing into two 7-inch lengths and two 3-inch lengths. Cover the wires by pushing the wire through the tubing. Leave both ends of all four wires uncovered.

Using the two shorter wires, connect the head and body of the stork. Push the wires into the Styrofoam far enough so that the bare wire is hidden.

The beak is formed by cutting one 6-inch length and one 4-inch length of pink chenille stem. Fold each piece into a V shape. The larger V shape is the upper beak. Put glue on the ends of the stems and push into the Styrofoam head in position for the mouth.

Cut two ovals from the black felt as a backing for the wiggle eyes. Glue the eyes onto the felt and then glue the felt onto the plastic.

To make the hat, cut a 3-inch circle from the poster board. Spread glue on one side of the poster board and press onto the black felt. Now spread glue on the other side of the poster board and fold the felt over. Smooth out the material and trim the felt around the posterboard. Next flatten the 1¼-inch ball on two opposite sides to form the crown of the hat. Glue black felt onto the crown and glue the crown onto the hat brim. Let dry. Glue the feather onto the hat. Position the hat on the stork's head and hold in place with glue.

Cut 19 inches of the pink gingham ribbon to measure 1 inch wide and glue it around the edge of the 6-inch disc. Then glue a 19-inch strip of blue ribbon in the center of the pink ribbon.

Cut the remaining pink ribbon into two 1-yard lengths. Trim one yard to measure 1 inch wide and leave the other yard regular size. Glue the blue ribbon in the center of the pink ribbon and let dry. Make two bows and secure with half of the pink chenille stem. Insert the stem of the wider bow into the center of the 6-inch disc. Insert the other bow into the Styrofoam at the stork's neck.

Push the longer wires into the Styrofoam behind the bow in the 6-inch disc, with 3 inches between them. Now push the stork onto his legs. It will be necessary to balance his weight, so do not push the legs all the way into the body the first time. If necessary, move the stork toward the center of the disc to maintain his balance.

Glue ribbon around the outside of the 10-inch Styrofoam disc. Curl the chenille stems around a pencil. Secure one end of a stem into the ring, glue it around the top edge, and push the other end into the ring. Continue to cover the outer edge with chenille stems. Glue the smaller stork base in the center of the larger base for better support.

❧ 18 ❧

CHILD'S BIRTHDAY

· *Party Invitation* ·

To start off your circus party theme, first commandeer a little help from the birthday child to make clown invitations for friends (Fig. 18-1).

MATERIALS

5½" x 8½" white construction paper
5½" x 8½" lime green burlap
3 orange chenille stems
2" x 2" flesh-colored felt
½" x 1" brown fake fur
red tri-bead
½" x ½" black felt

two 4mm white pearls
1" x 1½" red felt
3" of 2"-wide (#16) white ribbon with green polka dots
6" of ⅞"-wide (#5) orange ribbon with white polka dots
4 orange tri-beads
white glue

INSTRUCTIONS

Spread glue on one side of the construction paper. Lay the burlap onto the glue, smooth out the wrinkles, and press the burlap into the glue. Fold the burlap and paper in half, trim the paper and burlap for a smooth edge. Cut the orange chenille stems to fit the edges of the front. Glue the chenille pieces in place to form a border on the front.

Cut a 2-inch circle from the flesh-colored felt. Glue the circle on the front of the invitation, centered from the sides and one inch from the bottom edge. Pull several strands of fake fur from their backing. Arrange and glue the fur around the top of the circle to resemble hair. Glue the red tri-bead in the center of the circle for a nose. Cut two ¼ inch by ¼ inch triangles from the black felt and glue in position for eyes. Glue a white pearl in the center of each piece of black felt. Cut a mouth shape from the red felt, following the pattern in Figure 18-2, and glue in position.

Cut a triangular shape for the hat from the white ribbon, following the pattern in Figure 18-2. Glue the hat in position, just covering the edge of the hair. Cut a hat brim, ³⁄₁₆ by 3¼ inches, from the orange

*Fig. 18-1 Drum Favor, Clown Glass, Teddy Bear Mirror,
invitation, Clown, and Clown Pin.*

Fig. 18-2 Hat and mouth patterns for the clown invitation.

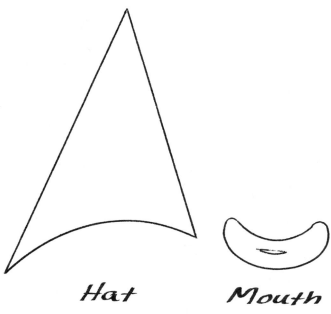

Hat   Mouth

ribbon to fit the bottom of the hat and glue in position. Glue three orange tri-beads on the hat. Cut a bow-tie shape 2¼ inches long from the orange ribbon and glue in position at the neckline. Glue the remaining orange tri-bead in position for a bow tie knot.

Fill out the invitation and you're ready with party favors and centerpieces.

· Circus Favors ·

The next three projects, all shown in Figure 18-1, are ideas for party favors that young visitors would love to have as keepsakes.

· CLOWN PIN ·

MATERIALS

1½"-diameter wooden disc
1" pin back
1½" yellow chenille stem
¼" x ½" red felt
1½" x 1½" orange ribbon with
    white polka dots

1 orange tri-bead
brown fake fur
black felt-tip pen
white paint
scissors
white glue

INSTRUCTIONS

Paint the wooden disc white; allow it to dry. Glue the pin back on the disc, just above center.

Pull strands of fake fur from their backing and arrange them around the top of the disc to resemble hair, then glue in place.

Using the black felt-tip pen, sketch triangular-shaped eyes and nose. Cut a 1¼ by 1 inch triangular shape from the orange ribbon, then glue in position for a hat. Glue the yellow chenille stem in position for a hat brim. Glue the tri-bead at the peak of the hat.

Cut a mouth shape from the red felt and glue in position. Your pin is now ready for all the partygoers.

· CLOWN PARTY GLASS ·

MATERIALS

10-ounce clear plastic tumbler
two 12mm blue glass ovals
one 16mm brown glass oval

one 16mm red glass circle
white glue

INSTRUCTIONS

Glue the red glass circle halfway up on the outside of the tumbler.

Glue the brown oval in position for a mouth, and the blue ovals in position for eyes—voilà!

· DRUM FAVOR ·

MATERIALS

2½"-diameter x 2"-high tin can
  with snap-on lid
2" x 9" orange burlap
3" x 6" lime green burlap
18" green gimp

16" yellow soutache
orange chenille stem
scissors
white glue

INSTRUCTIONS

Spread glue around the side of the can. Wrap the orange burlap around the can, smoothing out the wrinkles as you go, pressing the burlap into the glue. Place glue under the end of the burlap to hold it in place.

Spread glue on one end of the can, press the green burlap into the glue. Trim the burlap around the edge. Glue and trim the green burlap to the other end of the can.

Cut two pieces of gimp to the correct length for fitting around the can. Spread glue on the back of the gimp and wrap one piece around the can at the top and the other at the bottom to form bands.

Make a zigzag pattern between the bands with the yellow soutache, as shown in Figure 18-1, and hold in place with glue. Cut two 2½-inch pieces from the orange chenille stem and glue in place on top for drumsticks.

· Clown ·

The clown with his balloons (Fig. 18-1) will lead off your circus parade.

MATERIALS

6"-high Styrofoam cone
2½" Styrofoam egg
three 1¼"-diameter Styrofoam
  balls
1"-diameter Styrofoam ball
3½ yd royal blue 3"-bump chenille
3 yd lime green 3"-bump chenille
2 orange chenille stems
1 yd royal blue soutache
1 yd of 2¾"-wide (#40) white
  ribbon with green polka dots
4" x 4" black felt
2" x 2" red felt

3 yellow ball fringes
4" x 5" yellow fake fur
two 4mm pearl beads
two 2" pearl-headed pins
10mm red bead
4" x 4" poster board
white glue
scissors
serrated-edge knife
pencil
yellow spray paint
green spray paint

INSTRUCTIONS

To make legs for the clown, use a serrated knife to cut a one-inch-wide by three-inch-long slice out of the bottom of the Styrofoam cone.

Cut all the blue and green chenille into single bumps. Starting at the edge of the pant legs, push one end of a blue bump into the bottom of the cone and bend up toward the top of the cone. Push the other end into the Styrofoam. Make a row around each leg, *alternating* blue and green bumps. When the legs are complete, make a second row above the legs, starting at the ends of the bumps already in place. Finish covering the cone by wrapping the top with four or five green bumps. Be sure the cone is completely covered, with no Styrofoam showing through.

Use 18 inches of polka-dot ribbon for a collar. Cut it to 2 inches wide. Run a gathering thread along one edge and pull up tight to a diameter of 4 inches. Glue and pin the collar to the very top of the cone.

Cut the 1-inch Styrofoam ball in half. Then cut a small wedge out of each half to shape a hand. Push the cut ends of *two* blue chenille bumps into the edge of each hand. Then stick the other end of the two bumps into the cone right under the collar. Shape the bumps to resemble arms.

Glue the three yellow fringes down the front for buttons. Cut two shoes (Fig. 18-3) from poster board and cover both sides with black felt. Glue in place at the bottom of the legs.

Cut a 3-inch circle from the poster board. Glue to the ribbon and trim. Repeat to cover the other side. Cut the cone for the hat from ribbon, following the pattern in Figure 18-3, and glue the seams. Then put glue on the bottom edge of the cone and glue to the center of the hat brim. Set aside to dry.

Flatten the large end of the egg—this will be the top of his head. Cut the clown's eyes from black felt and the mouth from red felt. Glue

Fig. 18-3 Hat and shoe patterns for Clown.

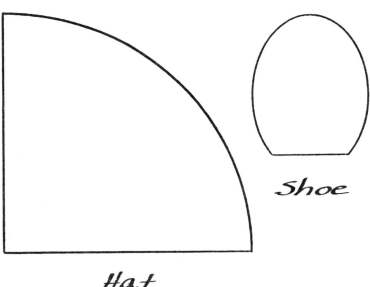

Shoe

Hat

in place. Glue the pearl beads in the center of the black felt for eyes. Glue the red bead in position for a nose. Comb the fake fur, then glue and pin it in position with the 5-inch length going from ear to ear.

Push a 2-inch piece of chenille stem into the head at the neckline. Now put glue on the top end of the Styrofoam cone and push the chenille stem into the cone to hold the head in place. Wrap one blue chenille bump around the neck above the collar.

Glue blue soutache around the edge of the hat brim and around the base of the crown (Fig. 18-1). Glue one blue bump on top of the hat. Push a 2-inch pearl pin through the hat and into the head to hold the hat in position. You might want to put some glue on the bottom of the hat also.

Spray one 1¼-inch-diameter Styrofoam ball with green paint and another with yellow, leaving one white. Cut the orange chenille stems into 3-inch, 4-inch, and 4½-inch lengths. Push one stem piece into each ball. Tie three bows, each with 6 inches of blue soutache and glue one bow on each stem next to the ball. Push the ends of the stems into the clown's left hand. Push the other 2-inch pearl pin into hand and body to hold them in place. Now he's holding the balloons high in the air.

· Birthday Circus Wagon ·

The birthday parade wagon with the lion and his tiny cake and presents is shown in the color section, Figure 14. The project is made in three parts.

· WAGON ·

MATERIALS

8″ x 12″ Styrofoam block, 1″ thick
8 yd yellow loopy chenille
4 yellow chenille stems
1¼ yd of ⅞″-wide (#5) green
   ribbon with white polka dots
2¼ yd gold single-loop braid
6″ x 6″ cardboard

6″ x 12″ orange felt
four 2″ pearl-headed pins
4 white bell-shaped beads
2¼ yd yellow velvet tubing
straight pins
scissors
white glue

INSTRUCTIONS

Start making the wagon by spreading glue in a 3-inch-wide strip along the length of the Styrofoam block on one flat surface. Let the glue set for 3 to 4 minutes. Now, begin in one of the glued corners and lay the yellow loopy chenille in a line along the edge of the block. Press the chenille firmly into the glued surface. Do not cut the chenille at the end of the row: bend it and lay a second row snugly against the first row, completely covering the Styrofoam surface. Remember to press the chenille into the glue. Continue placing and pressing the chenille in rows until the glued surface is covered.

Spread glue over another 3-inch-wide strip and continue, repeating the gluing and placing of chenille until one side of the Styrofoam block is completely covered.

Spread glue on the edges of the Styrofoam block. Place the green ribbon with white polka dots on the glued surface, continuing around the Styrofoam until the edge is completely covered. Trim off any excess ribbon.

Using a toothpick, spread a thin line of glue along the top edge of the ribbon. Now, place the gold braid onto the glue. Be sure that the loops are toward the yellow surface, extending over the edge of the ribbon. Next, spread glue on the bottom edge of the ribbon and put another row of gold braid in place.

Cut four 3-inch circles out of the cardboard. Spread glue on one side of each cardboard circle and place the glued sides onto the orange felt. Trim the felt around the cardboard circles. Cover the other side of each circle with glue, place each onto the remaining felt, and trim away the excess.

Cut the yellow chenille stems into 3-inch lengths. Glue four lengths of chenille stem onto one side of each circle to resemble the spokes of a wheel. Spread glue on the edge of the wheel and place the yellow tubing in the glue. Trim the tubing to the correct length. Place a bell-shaped bead onto a pearl-headed pin. Push the pin through the center of the wheel—where the chenille stems cross—and then into the edge of the Styrofoam, 2½ inches from one end. Attach the other three wheels in the same manner, placing each one 2½ inches from a corner.

· LION ·

MATERIALS

2″-diameter Styrofoam ball
2½″ Styrofoam egg
5 yd yellow and brown variegated
   3″-bump chenille
1 black ball fringe
½″ x ½″ brown felt

two 10mm wiggle eyes
5 round toothpicks
½″ x 12″ rust-colored fake fur
scissors
white glue

INSTRUCTIONS

Cut the yellow and brown chenille into one double bump for the tail and all the remainder into single bumps for the body. Put one end of a single bump into the Styrofoam ball at any point: we will call this the *front*. Wrap the bump around the Styrofoam and insert the other end into the opposite side of the ball: the *back*. Use fifteen bumps to cover the ball. This will be the lion's head.

Next, take one bump and center it on the space in front where the ends of the other bumps meet. Hold the bump in place and push both ends into the Styrofoam. Cover the corresponding space on the back in the same manner. Now glue the black ball fringe onto the bump in the center front for his nose. Cut a triangular-shaped mouth from the brown felt and glue just below the nose. Glue the wiggle eyes in position above the nose. For each ear, form a loop with a single bump, pushing the ends into the Styrofoam in position above the eyes. The ears should be further apart than the eyes.

Cover the Styrofoam egg in the same manner as the ball. Start in the center of the wider end and use fifteen bumps to cover the egg. Cover the space in the center of the wide end with a single bump. To make the legs, wrap a chenille bump around half the length of a toothpick. Push the uncovered end of the toothpick into the Styrofoam in position for a leg. Repeat three times. Use the double bump to make the tail. Loop one bump and pull it into a loosely tied knot. Push the other end of the double bump into the wide end of the Styrofoam egg in position for a tail.

To join the head and body, push a toothpick halfway into the side of the head, just below the level of the nose. Holding the head, push the other half of the toothpick into the body at the space where the bump ends meet on the narrow end of the egg. Wrap a chenille bump around his neck and push the ends into the Styrofoam. Place the fake fur around his face and behind his ears forming a magnificent mane for your lion. Use glue and pins to hold in place.

To complete the Birthday Circus Wagon, place the cake, gifts, and lion in position on the wagon.

· BIRTHDAY CAKE AND PRESENTS ·

MATERIALS

2½"-diameter Styrofoam disc, 1" thick
2 yd white curly chenille
"Happy Birthday" cake trim
5 birthday candles
2¼" x 3½" Styrofoam block, 1" thick
⅔ yd of ⅞"-wide (#5) green ribbon with white polka dots
⅓ yd of ⅞"-wide (#5) white ribbon with green polka dots
½ yd of ⅞"-wide (#5) orange ribbon with white polka dots
1¾ yd yellow soutache
scissors
serrated-edge knife
white glue

INSTRUCTIONS

Spread glue on one flat side of the disc to begin the cake. Start the white curly chenille at the center of the glued surface. Turn the chenille into a closely spaced spiral, pressing it into the glue. Continue turning and gluing the chenille until the surface is covered. Do not cut the chenille. Next, spread glue around the edge of the disc. Continue placing the chenille in rows, wrapping around the disc until the edge is covered. Cut off the excess. Cut the candles in half. Arrange the candles and the "Happy Birthday" trim on top of the cake.

To make the assortment of presents, first cut the Styrofoam block into five pieces: two pieces ½ by 1 by 2 inches; two pieces ¾ by 1 by 2¼ inches; and one piece 1 by 1 by 1 inch. Cover the two large pieces of Styrofoam, using the green ribbon with white polka dots. Spread glue on the Styrofoam and press the ribbon onto the glue. Trim off the excess ribbon. Cover one medium-sized piece and the small piece of Styrofoam using the orange ribbon with white polka dots. Use the white ribbon with green polka dots to cover the remaining medium-sized piece of Styrofoam. Next, tie the five packages using the yellow soutache for ribbon and bow material.

· Birthday Circus Cage ·

The centerpiece shown in Figure 14 (color section) is made in three parts, as was the Circus Wagon.

· TIGER ·

MATERIALS

5 yd orange and black variegated 3″-bump chenille
2″-diameter Styrofoam ball
2½″ Styrofoam egg
two 10mm wiggle eyes

6mm red bead
5 round toothpicks
scissors
white glue

INSTRUCTIONS

Cut the orange and black chenille into single bumps. Using the single bumps and the Styrofoam ball, construct the tiger's head by following the directions previously given for the lion. (*See* Birthday Circus Wagon, preceding project). Glue the red bead in the center front for his nose. Next, glue the wiggle eyes in position just above the nose. Each ear is formed by shaping a single bump into a loop. Push the ends of the loop into the Styrofoam in position above the eyes. The ears should be placed further apart than the eyes.

The body is made by covering the Styrofoam egg with chenille bumps, also following the directions for the lion's body. The legs are formed by wrapping a chenille bump around one-half the length of a toothpick. Push the uncovered end of the toothpick into the Styrofoam in position for a leg. Repeat for each leg. A single chenille bump is used for the tail. Push one end of the bump into the large end of the Styrofoam in position, then shape the chenille.

The head and body are joined by pushing a toothpick halfway into the side of the head, just below the level of the nose. Holding the head, push the other half of the toothpick into the body at the space where the chenille bump ends meet on the narrow end of the egg.

· GORILLA ·

MATERIALS

2″ Styrofoam egg	¼″ x ¼″ orange felt
1½″-diameter Styrofoam ball	straight pins
3 yd brown curly chenille	round toothpick
5 brown 3″-bump chenille	scissors
two 7mm wiggle eyes	white glue

INSTRUCTIONS

The gorilla's body is formed by covering the Styrofoam egg with the brown curly chenille. Start by spreading glue over the wider end, covering half of the egg. Place the end of the curly chenille in the center of the large end of the egg. Hold the chenille in place by pushing a straight pin through the chenille into the Styrofoam. Now, wrap the chenille in a spiral around the egg, placing each row snugly against the last and pressing the chenille into the glue. Use pins to hold the chenille in place as required. Continue wrapping until the glued area is covered. Set aside to dry.

Now spread glue over the remainder of the Styrofoam egg. Continue wrapping the chenille around the egg until the Styrofoam is completely covered. Cut the chenille and trim the end to fit neatly onto the narrow end of the egg. Use four brown 3-inch bumps of chenille for his arms and legs. Push one end of each bump into the Styrofoam in position and shape the chenille.

The head is made by covering the Styrofoam ball with the curly brown chenille. Spread glue over half of the ball. Place the end of the curly chenille in the middle of the glued area. Hold the chenille in place with a pin. Wrap and cover the ball, following the directions for the body. Cut the orange felt into the shape of a mouth. Fasten in place with glue. Glue the wiggle eyes in position just above the mouth. Cut the remaining 3-inch chenille bump in half, and form each piece into a loop. Push the ends of the loop into the Styrofoam in position for his ears.

The head and body are joined together by pushing the toothpick halfway into the head and then pushing the other half into the narrow end of the body.

· CAGE ·

MATERIALS

two 8″ x 12″ Styrofoam blocks,
  each 1″ thick
8 yd green loopy chenille
4 yellow chenille stems
7 yellow jumbo chenille stems
2½ yd of ⅞″-wide (#5) orange
  ribbon with white polka dots
3″ of ⅞″-wide (#5) white ribbon
  with green polka dots
4½ yd gold single-loop braid

6″ x 6″ cardboard
6″ x 12″ green felt
12″ x 16″ orange felt
2¼ yd yellow velvet tubing
five 2″ pearl-headed pins
4 white bell-shaped beads
straight pins
scissors
white glue

INSTRUCTIONS

The cage is constructed by first building the bottom piece, complete with wheels, then making the top and joining the two pieces together with the jumbo chenille bars.

The bottom piece is built following the same directions as the Birthday Circus Wagon (*See* previous project in this chapter). One side of a Styrofoam block is covered with *green* loopy chenille. The edges of the Styrofoam are covered with the orange polka-dot ribbon and trimmed with the gold braid. The wheels are made using the green felt and are fastened to the Styrofoam with the pearl-headed pins.

Use the second Styrofoam block for the top. Cut the orange felt into two 8 by 12 inch pieces. Spread glue on one side of the Styrofoam. Lay one piece of felt onto the glue, smooth out wrinkles, stretch and trim the felt to meet the edges, and press the felt into the glue. Set aside to dry. Next glue the remaining felt to the other side of the Styrofoam. Following the procedure for the bottom piece, cover the edges of Styrofoam with ribbon and trim with the gold braid.

Cut the jumbo chenille stems in half so that you have fourteen pieces. These will be the bars for the cage. Place one bar at each corner of the bottom piece and push into the Styrofoam so that they stand upright. Next, space three bars evenly along each side and two bars on each end, pushing these pieces into the Styrofoam so that they stand up straight.

Place the tiger and the gorilla in the cage. Set the top piece onto the ends of the bars. Space the bars evenly, then push the ends into the Styrofoam. Be sure that the bars are straight and even and that the top is level.

Cut a triangular-shaped flag out of the 3-inch piece of white polka-dot ribbon. Glue the short edge of the ribbon to the remaining pearl-headed pin and stick it into the roof.

· Teddy Bear Mirror ·

Any little boy or girl will be delighted to hang this mirror, shown in Figure 18-1, in their room. Be sure it hangs at the right height to be useful. The bear can be made in any color—to match individual room decorations.

MATERIALS

34 yd brown 3″-bump chenille
4 white 3″chenille bumps
1 red 5″ chenille bump
brown chenille stem
6″-diameter Styrofoam disc, 1½″ thick
9″-diameter Styrofoam disc, 1½″ thick

three 2½″-diameter Styrofoam balls
1″ x 2″ black felt
5″-diameter round mirror
4 wooden craft sticks
scissors
serrated-edge knife
white glue

INSTRUCTIONS

Lay the mirror in the center of the 9-inch Styrofoam disc. Mark a line around the outside edge of mirror with a black felt-tip pen. Put the mirror aside.

Cut all the brown chenille into single bumps. Be sure to cut the chenille through the smallest diameter area. Bend all the bumps into U shapes. Starting along the outside of the marked circle on the 9-inch disc, push both ends of a brown loop into the Styrofoam. Give the loop a twist halfway around, and bend the loop over so that it is against the Styrofoam. Continue placing loops around the circle until you have completed one row. Now place a second, then a third, row to the outside of the first. This should bring you to the edge of the disc. Next cover the outside edge of the disc; two rows of loops should be enough.

Spread glue on the back of the mirror. Press the glued side down in the open center of the 9-inch disc. Set aside to dry.

Locate the center of the 6-inch Styrofoam disc. Push one brown chenille bump into the center. Now make four rows of loops around the center. If you need a fifth row to bring you to the edge of the disc, add it. Cover the outside edge of the disc with two rows of brown bump chenille.

Break the craft sticks in half. Push two pieces of craft stick into the edge of the large disc, one inch apart. Put glue on the other ends. Now push the glued ends into one edge of the 6-inch disc, thus joining the head and body of the bear.

Cut the three Styrofoam balls in half with a serrated knife: these six pieces will make ears and paws for the bear. Completely cover the rounded side of each piece with brown loops, then cover each flat side.

Use the remaining craft sticks to attach the four paws and two ears in appropriate positions—see the bear's picture, Figure 18-1.

Fig. 18-4 Eye pattern for Teddy Bear Mirror.

Bend the red bump into a U shape and push into the top Styrofoam disc as a mouth.

Cut the white bump chenille into two pieces, two bumps each. Fold each in the middle and glue in position for eyes. Cut black felt for eyes, following the pattern in Figure 18-4, and glue onto the white bump chenille.

Bend the 4-inch pieces of chenille stem into a U shape. Put glue on both ends and insert in the Styrofoam at the top center of the back as a hanger.

❧ 19 ❧

FATHER'S BIRTHDAY

· *Centerpiece and Table Setting* ·

This personalized table setting, shown in the color section in Figure 15, is perfect for the celebration dinner on father's special day.

MATERIALS

Decotique no. 73 "Autumn Owls"
paper place mat
plate, cup, and napkin
two 6″ x 10″ sheets gold
   construction paper
3″ x 4″ gold construction paper
14″ x 22″ brown paper
wooden mushroom basket

wooden candy container
cream-colored acrylic paint
black felt-tip marker
acrylic sealer
½″ paint brush
scissors
gesso
two 3″-diameter gold candles

INSTRUCTIONS

Paint the mushroon basket with two coats of gesso and two coats of cream-colored paint. Read the manufacturer's label for drying time. When it's dry, you're ready to apply the Decotiques. Detailed instructions are given under Fourth of July Picnic (*See* Ch. 9)

To personalize the basket centerpiece and give it extra usage, use the felt-tip pen to print the following message around the top edge:

When the party is over, keep your odd socks in
here and we'll try to match them.

When thoroughly dry, protect the Decotiques and printing with one coat of clear varnish or sealer. Let this dry and fill with fruit.

Give the candles a coat of sealer; otherwise the wax will resist the transfers. Allow to dry and apply Decotiques. I used the group of three owls on one candle and a pair of owls on the other. Also put mushroom candle rings around the candles.

My suggestion for the plate is one of the large owls; for the napkin, a small owl; for the cup, the mushroom and mice; and for the place mat, mushrooms.

Put a protective coating of sealer on the plate so the guest of honor can have it as a keepsake. To further protect it, I suggest using an undecorated plate over it when eating.

Paint and finish the candy container in the same manner as the mushroom basket. When dry, rub on the mushroom designs and seal.

Fold the three sheets of construction paper in half. Use the small one as a place card, rubbing on a tiny owl transfer at one end. Use the barrel and wagon wheel motif on a large card as the invitation. Put a big owl on the other and use as the gift card.

The hat, made out of a large piece of brown wrapping paper, 14 inches by 22 inches, is a simple folding process:

1. Fold in half to form a double thickness, 11 by 14 inches

2. On the folded side, fold each corner over at a 45° angle so that the first fold meets at the center

3. Now turn up the flaps at the open end, each to the outside, to form a headband

Use odds and ends of Decotiques to decorate.

· Owl Clock ·

The clock shown in color, Figure 15, utilizes a purchased mechanism; the rest of the gift is handmade.

MATERIALS

7⅞" x 7½" x 3" wooden box
Decotique No. 73 "Autumn Owls"
polymer medium (acrylic finish)
nylon brush
cream-colored acrylic paint
white acrylic paint
clock mechanism

3 yd paper braid
7⅞" x 7½" glass
balsa strips
#400 sandpaper
hardware, hinges, ball feet, catch, ring

INSTRUCTIONS

Sand the box and wipe dust away with damp paper towel. Reverse the lid and paint it with white paint. Paint the rest of the box the cream color. Apply two coats and, when dry, sand with #400 sandpaper. Then apply the final base coat.

Cut out the owls from the center of each Decotique sheet. Position one owl at the center of the reversed box lid white side down, and rub all over with applicator. Peel away the backing paper. Cut and position the ears of corn around the central owl and use the ladybugs as the hour signs of the clock. Use the oak leaves as borders, the mushrooms on the sides, and the pumpkins for the top. Position the other owl on the outside bottom of the box.

Apply gold braid around the edges and then brush on two coats of polymer medium.

Attach the clock mechanism to the back side of the lid, making sure that the spindle is at the center of your numerals. Secure clock hands to the spindle.

Finally affix the hardware: ring pull at top, hinge to left side, and catch to opposite side, ball feet to the bottom of box.

Note: If glass is to be used, cut the balsa strips to fit inside edges of reversed lid of box, leaving ¼ inch to the rim. Do this prior to painting the box. Take the box lid to your glass supplier and have him cut the glass to exact size. Follow all instructions to complete the box and finally glue in the glass, so that it rests on the balsa strips. Apply braid to cover the edges of the glass.

Now with the gift completed, start planning your menu! Have a good time!

SILVER ANNIVERSARY

· *Anniversary Centerpiece* ·

The gala anniversary centerpiece is shown in Figure 20-1.

MATERIALS

driftwood base
white spray paint
nine 18″ lengths #16 stem wire
white floral tape
2″ x 2″ Styrofoam block
1 yd of 6″-wide white netting
3 yd of #28 wire
1½ dozen silver leaves

14 yd silver tinsel tex wire
2″-diameter jar
9 yd $^5/_{16}$″-wide (#1½) white
 acetate ribbon
lacy "25" paper cutout
scissors
#618 glue

INSTRUCTIONS

Spray the driftwood base with white paint. Let dry.

Wrap all the 18-inch pieces of stem wire with white floral tape. Then wrap three stems together for half (9 inches) of their length. This is the tree trunk. Bend two of the wires for limbs, leaving the third upright. Add the remaining wires to the third wire, one at a time, and secure with tape to make the branches of the tree. Carefully shape each branch.

Glue the Styrofoam block onto the top surface at one end of your driftwood base. Let dry. Then push the wire tree into the Styrofoam.

Gather the netting in the center and tie with a 4-inch piece of #28 wire. Arrange it around the base of tree and push the wire into Styrofoam. Glue three silver leaves under the edge of the net.

Now we'll make the flowers. Wrap tinsel tex wire around the jar seven times, then cut the wire. Slide the circles of wire off the glass and pinch together at the center, twisting to make a figure eight. Wrap a 9-inch piece of tinsel tex wire around the center twice, leaving one long end. Now wrap this around a pencil to make a coil center for the flower.

Fig. 20-1 Silver Anniversary centerpiece and matching candleholders.

Using 32 inches of ribbon, make a bow. Secure the center with a piece of #28 wire. Lay the bow on top of the silver leaves and lay the wire flower on top of that. Tie these together with a 5-inch piece of #28 wire. Then wire this to a branch. I used eight flowers, placing them at random on the branches.

Make another bow and tie it to the "25" cutout. Glue this at the base of the tree.

You might like to put names of the guests of honor on the driftwood, too.

· Silver Candleholders ·

The candleholders shown in Figure 20-1 are a perfect complement to the centerpiece.

two 6"-diameter Styrofoam discs
  1" thick
spray adhesive
silver glitter
clear acrylic spray glaze
3 yd of ⁵⁄₁₆"-wide (#1½) white
  acetate ribbon

3 yd silver tinsel tex wire
4 silver leaves
10" of #28 wire
1 yd of 6"-wide white netting
scissors
two 12" white candles

INSTRUCTIONS

Remember to lay newspapers on the floor when using spray adhesive.
Spray both discs on one side and around the edges. Hold a disc over a
lid and sprinkle silver glitter onto the sprayed areas. Then pour excess
glitter back into the container. Do the other disc, then spray discs with
the glaze; this will help to hold the glitter in place. Glue ribbon around
the center of the edges.

Make two ribbon and tinsel tex flowers, following the directions for the
Anniversary Centerpiece. Also assemble the flowers, leaves, and bows
in the same way. Gather the netting and wire together with the flower
grouping. Push a candle into the center of a disc, about two-thirds of
the way through. Then push the netting arrangement into the
Styrofoam in front of the candle. Complete the other in the same way.

❧ 21 ❧

GOLDEN ANNIVERSARY

· *Hanging Basket* ·

Figure 21-1 shows the 50th anniversary centerpiece, a hanging basket adorned with doves.

MATERIALS

half of a 3″-diameter Styrofoam
  ball
12″ spherical metal frame
gold spray paint
3¼ yd of 6″-wide net
spray adhesive
gold glitter
gold chenille stem
10 gold tinsel stems
2 doves

1 dozen gold leaves
1 bunch white flowers
"50" gold medallion
2½ yd of 1⁷⁄₁₆″-wide (#9) gold
  lamé ribbon
white glue
scissors
measuring tape
newspapers

INSTRUCTIONS

Spread newspapers on the floor and spray the metal frame and the half ball with gold paint. Let dry.

Cut the net into 18-inch pieces. Hold the net over the newspaper and spray three pieces of netting with adhesive. Now work over a box lid, sprinkling gold glitter over the three net pieces. Set aside to dry. Pour extra glitter back into container.

Glue the half ball into the spherical wire frame at the point where all wires cross. For added security, bend half a chenille stem into a U shape and push into the ball across several wires.

Cut three tinsel stems in half: make a hanging chain with these. Attach to the top of the frame, opposite the Styrofoam. Hang up the frame so it's easier to work on.

Gather each piece of netting in the center and tie with a 4-inch piece of tinsel stem. Push one net puff into the Styrofoam at each section of frame. Alternate the plain and the glittered net.

Fig. 21-1 Hanging Basket for the Golden Anniversary.

Position one dove on each side of the Styrofoam. Place four gold leaves behind the doves. Position three leaves at the bottom of the Styrofoam and four around the sides.

Scatter the tiny white flowers around the Styrofoam. Use half a tinsel stem to suspend the "50" medallion from the center top.

Make a bow using all the ribbon and tie with a tinsel stem. Attach the bow to frame at the top. Glue a gold leaf in the center of the bow. Have the streamers hanging to each side.

This project could be done in silver for a 25th anniversary.

· BASKET FAVOR ·

The dainty basket shown in Figure 21-2 makes a charming favor for guests to keep.

MATERIALS

small basket
gold spray paint
9″ x 6″ white net
gold tinsel stem
small wedge of Styrofoam

24″ of ⁵/₁₆″-wide (#1½) white acetate ribbon
scissors
dinner mints

INSTRUCTIONS

Spray the basket with gold paint.

Gather the netting along the center and tie with a short piece of tinsel stem. Wedge a small piece of Styrofoam into the basket. Push the stem of the net into the Styrofoam.

Make a four-loop bow and secure at center with a 5-inch piece of tinsel stem. Push this into Styrofoam also. Fill the basket with mints.

Fig. 21-2 Basket favor for Fiftieth Anniversary party.

22

SWIM PARTY

·*Swim Trunks Invitation*·

These directions are for one invitation, shown in Figure 22-1.

MATERIALS

7″ white skirt zipper   scissors
4″ x 7″ purple construction paper   white glue
black felt-tip pen

INSTRUCTIONS

Following the pattern in Figure 22-2, cut one pair of trunks from con-struction paper. Fold the trunks on the fold lines. There will be a ½-inch space in the front of the trunks for the zipper. Before you insert the zipper, write your greeting inside the trunks with the felt-tip pen.

Pull the zipper open and cut off 3¾ inches from the top of the zipper. Zip up the zipper to ¼ inch from the end, so that the zipper pull does not come off.

Fig. 22-1 Life Preserver favor and Swim Trunks Invitation.

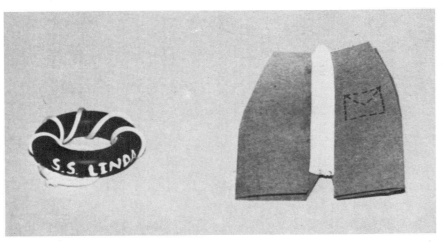

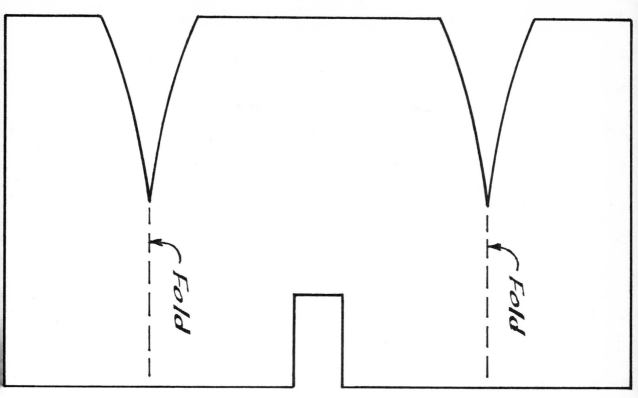

Fig. 22-2 Pattern for Swim Trunks Invitation.

Glue the zipper to the front seam. With the pen, draw a pocket on the right front of the trunks.

Who could resist such a delightful invitation?

· *Life Preserver* ·

The inner tube shown in Figure 22-1 serves as a napkin holder, place card, and party favor.

MATERIALS

1¼″-diameter wooden ring	small paint brush
black acrylic paint	½″ paint brush
white acrylic paint	scissors
30″ white satin macrame cord	white glue

INSTRUCTIONS

Paint the wooden ring black, using the larger brush. Let this dry thoroughly.

Using the small brush and white paint, print each guest's name on the side of one inner tube preceding it with S.S. if you wish. Let dry.

Glue one end of the cord to the right of the printed name. Wrap all but 12 inches of the cord around the ring until you reach the left side of the name. Glue the cord at that point. Roll up the remaining cord and tie the end of the cord around the roll (Fig. 22-1). Glue the roll at the left side of the name, making a life preserver.

· Linda's Swim Party ·

The poolside panorama in Figure 22-3 makes an appropriate and charming centerpiece for the buffet table.

MATERIALS

11" x 12" Styrofoam block, 1¼" thick
11" x 18" grass ribbon
47" of 1⁷/₁₆"-wide (#9) light green burlap ribbon
6" x 8" aluminum foil
6" x 8" light blue cellophane
28" white velvet tubing
aquarium gravel
white chenille stem
red chenille stem
three 12mm face beads
3 toothpicks
tongue depressor
12 wooden coffee stirrers
wood shavings
21" of 2"-high fencing

2" x 2" red felt
4" brown yarn
long pink balloon
miniature dog
waxed paper
orange acrylic paint
black acrylic paint
brown acrylic paint
blue acrylic paint
yellow acrylic paint
3" of ⅞"-wide (#5) yellow gingham ribbon
4" of 1⁷/₁₆"-wide (#9) red gingham ribbon
plastic individual cream servers (from a restaurant)
package of 3mm black beads

Fig. 22-3 Linda's Swim Party panoramic centerpiece.

2" x 2" net
#220 sandpaper
paint brush

scissors
Bread dough: 1 slice bread, lemon
juice, white glue

INSTRUCTIONS

Cut the grass ribbon to fit one 11- by 12-inch surface of the Styrofoam and glue in place. Trim the burlap ribbon to a width of 1¼ inches. Then, starting at one corner of the Styrofoam, glue the burlap ribbon around the edges.

Spread glue around the edges of the foil and place the cellophane onto the foil. When the glue dries, cut the foil into a standard pool shape such as an oval, a kidney shape, or a circle. Glue the edges of the shape together. Glue the foil to the grass about an inch from one long side of the block.

Glue the velvet tubing around the cellophane where it meets the grass. Cut off any excess tubing so that the ends meet exactly. Spread glue onto the grass next to the tubing to make a 1-inch border around the pool. Sprinkle aquarium gravel into the glue. To make sure the gravel stays in place, spread more glue on top of the gravel. Let this dry thoroughly.

To make the diving board, cut the tongue depressor to measure 3 inches long. Gently bend the depressor 1 inch from the *cut* edge. Paint the 1-inch length brown and glue wood shavings onto the 2-inch length. From the part of the depressor that remains cut a piece ½ inch long. Glue this to the bend in the diving board under the 2-inch length for the board support. Let this dry, then glue the support where the tubing and gravel meet at the "Deep end" of the pool.

To make the ladder, cut two 1-inch lengths of red chenille stem. Bend each piece into a U shape. Opposite the diving board, glue one end of each stem on either side of the tubing: that is, one end is glued to the gravel and one is glued to the cellophane. The stems should be ½ inch apart.

Glue the fence around three sides of the pool.

To make the picnic table, cut four coffee stirrers into 3-inch lengths so that you have eight pieces. Round the cut edges by sanding. Lay four pieces of the stirrers side by side on the waxed paper and glue them together. This is the surface of the table.

Round the edges of the other pieces you cut from the stirrers. Lay two pieces side by side on the waxed paper and glue together for the picnic bench. Repeat for a second bench.

For the table legs, cut four 1½-inch-long pieces from the stirrers. Glue two pieces together to make an X shape. Then make another X shape. Glue one pair of legs at each end of the table surface. You may need to hold the legs perpendicular to the table until the glue begins to dry.

For the bench legs, cut four ½-inch pieces of stirrer. Glue one piece to each end of each bench.

Glue the piece of red gingham ribbon to the table for the tablecloth. When all the glue dries, glue the picnic table and benches onto one corner of the grass.

For the lounge chair, cut three stirrers into 3-inch lengths. Gently bend three of the pieces 1 inch from the cut end for the chair back. Round the cut edges as before, by sanding. Lay the pieces side by side on waxed paper and glue together. Cut four ½-inch lengths of coffee stirrers and glue to the bottom of the chair for legs. Glue the yellow gingham ribbon to the chair surface. When all the glue dries, glue the chair onto the grass in the corner opposite to the table.

For the grill, you will use the bottom of the cream cup. Cut it to measure ¼ inch high. Paint the cup orange. When the paint dries, mark three spots on the bottom of the grill at even intervals. Punch holes at the marks with the point of your scissors. Cut the toothpicks to measure ¾ inches long and paint them black. Put glue on one end of each toothpick and push them into the holes for the legs of the grill. Spread glue inside the grill and sprinkle the black beads into the glue for charcoal. Glue the net to the top of the grill. When the glue dries, trim away excess net. Glue the miniature dog next to the grill.

To make the girl swimmer, cut off the tip of the balloon. Pull the tip over the top of one of the face beads and roll back the edge making her bathing cap. Glue the "neck" of the face onto the cellophane.

For the boy, cut an inch of yarn and unravel it. Glue it to one face bead for hair and glue the head to the cellophane.

For the sunbather, cut one piece of white chenille stem 3 inches long and another 2 inches long. Bend the longer piece in half. Push the bent end into the "neck" of the face bead for the body and legs. Wrap the 2-inch stem around the "body" and shape arms from it. Shape the legs. Style a bikini from the red felt and glue it onto the sunbather. Unravel the rest of the brown yarn and glue it onto the head for long hair. Then glue the girl onto the lounge chair.

To make the hot dogs, hamburgers, plates, and cups, you will use bread dough. Cut the crust from the slice of bread and tear the bread into tiny pieces. Hold the bread in one hand; add two teaspoons of glue and two drops of lemon juice. Roll and knead the mixture in your hands. At first, it will stick to your hands but after 5 or 6 minutes of mixing, it will all roll into a ball. Using about ¼ teaspoon for each piece, shape three cups, three plates, three hamburgers, and three hot dogs. As you form the dough pieces, set them on waxed paper and let them dry overnight. Store the excess dough in a plastic bag in the refrigerator and it will keep up to three weeks. When the shapes have dried, paint them.

You may glue the food and dishes where you please on the grill and table as soon as the paint dries.

23

LUAU

· *Pineapple Invitation* ·

Get your friends into the spirit for a luau with this appropriate invitation, shown in Figure 23-1.

MATERIALS

5″ x 11″ green construction paper
4″ of 4″-wide (#100) brown burlap
   ribbon

black felt-tip pen
scissors
white glue

INSTRUCTIONS

Using the pineapple pattern in Figure 23-2, cut out one pineapple from the green construction paper. Fold the paper on the folding line.

Using the same pattern for the fruit of the pineapple, cut one from the burlap ribbon. Glue the burlap to the side of the invitation that does *not* have leaves, to resemble the skin of a pineapple. Mark the burlap with scallops using the felt pen.

Be sure to include What, Where, and When so your friends can join you at the luau.

· *Polynesian Isle* ·

MATERIALS

11″ x 12″ Styrofoam block, 1¼″
   thick
4 yd brown loopy chenille
3 yd gold metallic string chenille
10 kelly green 5″ chenille bumps
6 kelly green 3″ chenille bumps

1 green chenille stem
1¼ yd 1⁷/₁₆″-wide (#9) green
   burlap ribbon
¼″ x 4″ gold felt
4″ x 4″ cardboard
wood shavings

Fig. 23-1 Polynesian Isle, palm tree favor, and invitation.

fold

Fig. 23-2 Half-size pattern for Pineapple Invitation. (To enlarge this pattern, first trace onto graph paper with 1″ squares. Then re-trace line-for-line onto 2″ square graph paper. This will bring the pattern up to full-size, ready for use.)

5 stems of small fabric flowers
6 small sweet gum balls (seed pods)
1 small seashell
1 large seashell
6″ dried pod
8″-high plastic doll

mustard-colored acrylic paint
coat hanger
scissors
serrated-edge knife
wire cutters
small paintbrush
white glue

INSTRUCTIONS

Using a serrated-edge knife, cut the Styrofoam block into a free-form shape to make the island base. Generously spread glue on one side of the base and sprinkle the wood shavings onto the wet glue. Allow to dry.

Spread glue around the edge of the base and press the green burlap into the glue. Smooth out the wrinkles as you place the ribbon, and trim to the correct length. Set aside to dry.

The palm tree is made from the coat hanger, loopy chenille and 5″-bump chenille. Cut a 14-inch length of wire from the coat hanger. Bend an inch at one end of the wire into a hook. Starting at the hooked end, wrap the loopy chenille around the wire to make the tree trunk. Completely cover the wire, except for an inch at the straight end. The wire in the loopy chenille should hold the chenille in place on the hanger wire. Leave the kelly green 5-inch bump chenille in one strand. Fold the bumps accordion style, bending at the narrow sections. With the two ends at the center, fan the double-bump loops out into a five-point star shape. Pinch the outer ends of the double loops tightly shut. At the center, pass the green chenille stem through the folded ends and twist the center together tightly. Be sure to place the loose ends of the bumps into the knot. Trim the ends of the stem close to the knot. Place the knot into the hook of the trunk. Arrange the leaves evenly around the hook, then pinch the hook shut to hold the leaves in place. Glue sweet gum balls—the seed pods from balsamiferous trees—underneath the leaves at the trunk to resemble coconuts. Place a glob of glue onto the uncovered end of the trunk. Position the trunk near one edge of the base and push the wire trunk into the Styrofoam.

Make three palm leaves, using the 3-inch bumps. Cut the chenille into three double bumps. Fold the double bumps and pinch the ends tightly. Place a dab of glue on the cut ends of the bumps and push the ends into the Styrofoam at the trunk of the tree. Shape the chenille to resemble leaves. Stick three stems of fabric flowers into the Styrofoam near the tree trunk. Set the small seashell near the flowers and hold in place with glue.

The girl's hula skirt is made using the string chenille, felt, and cardboard. Pin the felt along one edge of the cardboard. Spread glue onto the felt, being careful *not* to glue the felt to the cardboard. While the glue is wet, wrap the string chenille around the cardboard so that each strand is glued to the felt. Set aside to dry. Next, cut the loops at the end of the cardboard opposite the felt, unpin the felt and remove the skirt from the cardboard.

The floral lei is made by gluing small fabric flowers to string chenille. Cut a 4-inch length of string chenille, and cut the flowers off at the stems. Glue the flowers side by side on the string chenille. Glue the ends of the chenille together.

Paint a halter top on the doll. Glue three or four flowers in the doll's hair. Place the lei around her neck. Glue the felt top of the hula skirt around her waist. Set the girl under the tree and hold in place with glue. Arrange the large seashell and flower pod on the base and glue them in place, also.

· *Luau Favor* ·

Let's make a small palm tree, as shown in Figure 23-1, for everyone to take home.

MATERIALS

10 kelly green 2″ chenille bumps   floral adhesive
½ yard brown loopy chenille   wire cutters
small seashell   coat hanger

INSTRUCTIONS

Cut a piece from the coat hanger, 3½ inches long. Bend a ½-inch hook in one end. Wrap the loopy chenille around and around, completely covering the wire.

Leave the 2-inch bumps in one piece. Fold the bumps accordion style, bending at the narrow sections. With the two ends at the center, fan the double-bump loops out into a five-point star shape. Pinch the outer ends of the double loops shut. At the center, pass the green chenille stem through the folded ends and twist the center together tightly. Trim the ends of the stem.

Place the knot into the hook of the trunk. Arrange the leaves evenly and pinch the hook shut to hold the leaves in place.

Put a small glob of floral adhesive on the seashell and push the trunk wire into it. Pull some of the chenille yarn down over the floral adhesive for cover.

· *"Aloha"* ·

All you need now to complete your luau decor is a traditional South Seas greeting (Fig. 23-3).

13" x 18" yellow burlap
2½" x 11" light blue felt
3" x 11" gold felt
5" x 7" orange felt
7" x 8" green felt
2" x 3" light green felt

1²/₃ yd orange yarn
3" x 3" white felt
15" wooden dowel, ⅛" diameter
waxed paper
scissors
white glue

INSTRUCTIONS

Fringe a one-inch section of burlap along both of the longer sides and along one shorter side. The unfringed edge is the top.

Using the patterns, cut a large mountain (Fig. 23-4) from the green felt and a small mountain (Fig. 23-5) from the orange felt. Cut the larger snowcap (Fig. 23-4) from light green felt and the small snowcap (Fig. 23-5) from gold felt.

Along one 11-inch length of the light blue felt, cut three peaks to resemble waves (*See* Fig. 23-3). Cut seven whitecaps from the white felt. Along one 11-inch length of the gold felt, cut out shallow scallops in a random manner, attempting to make it resemble sand dunes.

Lay the burlap on waxed paper. Glue the straight side of the green mountain on the left side of the burlap, 2½ inches from the bottom edge. Be sure the side of the mountain does not cover the fringe. Now glue the straight side of the orange mountain on the right edge of the burlap, 2½ inches from the bottom edge. The left side of the orange mountain should overlap the green mountain about ⅛ inch, so that no gap occurs between the mountains.

Glue the light green snowcap on the green mountain and the gold snowcap on the orange mountain. Lay the scalloped gold felt to cover the bottom edge of each mountain, gluing it in place to resemble a beach.

Glue the blue waves below the gold sand so that the straight edge of the blue felt lies along the edge of the burlap fringe.

Glue a whitecap near the top of each wave, adding the others at random.

Following the pattern in Figure 23-6, trace "Aloha" onto the burlap. It should be at a 45° angle with the large *A* about an inch from the green mountain. The last *a* should be 3½ inches from the top of the burlap. Spread a thin line of glue over the lettering outline of the word. Then lay the yarn into the glue. Press very carefully into place. Cut away any excess yarn.

Fold over an inch of the unfringed end of the burlap and glue along the edge. When dry, slip the dowel into this slot. Tie one end of the remaining yarn onto each end of the dowel. When all the glue is dry, peel away the waxed paper. Put your hanging on the front door and you're ready to greet your friends Hawaiian style. Aloha!

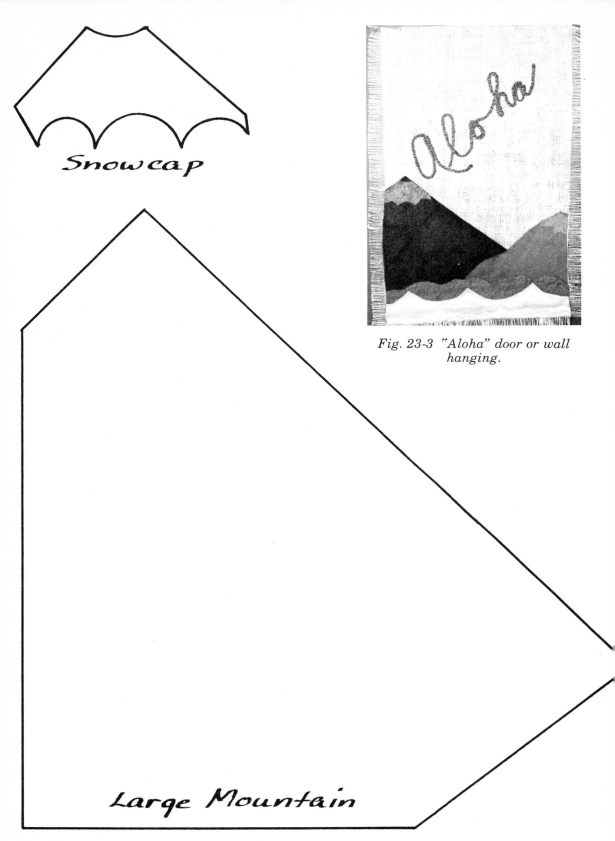

Snowcap

Fig. 23-3 "Aloha" door or wall hanging.

Large Mountain

Fig. 23-4 Pattern for large mountain and snowcap for "Aloha."

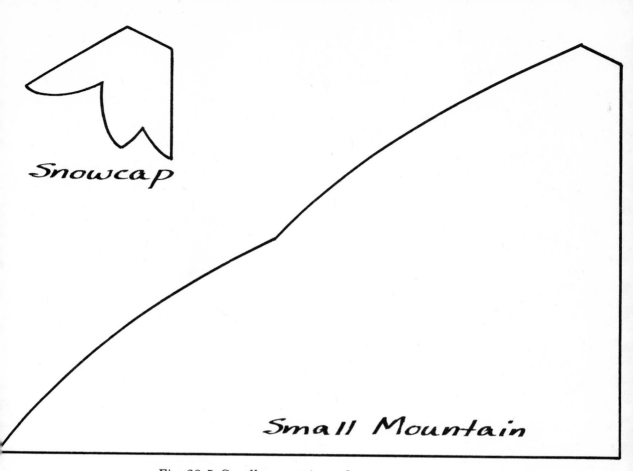

Snowcap

Small Mountain

Fig. 23-5 Small mountain and snowcap patterns.

Fig. 23-6 Lettering pattern for "Aloha" wall hanging.

176

⊰ 24 ⊱

FOR ANY OCCASION

· *Kitchen Vegetable Tree* ·

For any special occasion or a year-round centerpiece, try the vegetable tree—then the matching basket and ladle—shown in Figure 24-1.

MATERIALS

18″-high Styrofoam cone
4 dozen plastic parsley picks
2 dozen plastic assorted vegetable
   picks
6 green chenille stems

7 yd of ⅞″ wide (#5) green and
   white polka-dot ribbon
scissors
green spray paint

INSTRUCTIONS

Set the cone on newspapers and spray paint it green.

Cut short a few of the parsley pick stems. Push the stems into the Styrofoam along the bottom of the cone, side by side, halfway around. Now that you can see how to space them, cover the entire tree with parsley picks. If a piece falls off, twist a short piece of chenille stem around it and push into the Styrofoam. Space the greens so that the Styrofoam does not show, but do not overcrowd. Turn the tree around to be sure you've kept its shape; if not, adjust some of the greens.

Add the vegetables, putting six bunches around the bottom. Then alternate the next row, placing the picks in the spaces between the first row and about 4 inches above. Continue adding the vegetable picks until you're pleased with the arrangement. Save a tiny mushroom or radish for the top.

Cut twelve 18-inch pieces of ribbon. Make all into bows, securing the centers with 3-inch pieces of chenille stem. Place the bows at random all over the tree. Make a bow from the remaining ribbon and put it at top of the tree, with the streamers hanging to either side. Stick the tiny vegetable you saved in the center of bow.

Your pretty tree is ready for the kitchen table!

Fig. 24-1 Bread Basket, Kitchen Vegetable Tree, and Decorative Ladle.

· Bread Basket ·

To complement the kitchen vegetable tree, I used an old bread basket belonging to my mother.

MATERIALS

1 plastic mushroom pick
2 plastic teafern picks
2½ yd of ⅞"-wide (#5) green
   and white polka-dot ribbon

11"-diameter basket
scissors
white glue

INSTRUCTIONS

Weave the ribbon through the sides of the basket. Cut off the extra ribbon and glue the ends to the inside of the basket. Repeat for a second row (Fig. 24-1).

Push the stems of the teafern picks through the basket over the seams of the ribbon. Twist the wires together inside the basket and cut off the extra wire.

Make a bow from the ribbon and attach to the basket in the center of the greens. Fasten the mushroom pick in the center of the bow. Put a napkin and bread in the basket and you're ready for your guests.

· Decorative Ladle ·

While wandering through the hardware store one day, I found this painted ladle (Fig. 24-1). I thought it would fit in with the kitchen vegetable tree and bread basket.

MATERIALS

1½ dozen miniature artificial fruits	white glue
	scissors
24″ of ⅜″-wide (#1½) red ribbon	#28 wire
6″ ladle	

INSTRUCTIONS

Cut the wires from the artificial fruits. Arrange fruits in the bowl of the ladle and glue in place.

While this dries, make a bow from the ribbon, tying at center with the wire. Leave the ends of the wire to the back of the ribbon. Use them to attach bow to ladle handle and to use as a hanger.

· Decalon Plates ·

INSTRUCTIONS

Decalon is a new craft material used to transfer pictures to paper, wood, eggs, glass, etc. The adhesive-backed plastic film is practically indestructible. It is much faster than other transfer mediums, does not require a final coat, and you have a washable surface. You can use Decalon with any card, print, wrapping paper, etc. Liftable prints are also available, printed on a special paper. Using Decalon and Liftable prints, your transfer is finished in 5 minutes. I've really had fun working with Decalon—the plates in Figure 24-2 are an example of the projects you can make.

Cut a piece of Decalon slightly smaller than your print. Have your print face up on a hard surface, such as Masonite. Start at a corner, and very carefully remove the brown backing paper from the Decalon.

Fig. 24-2 *Plates decorated with prints and Decalon transfer materials.*

Put the sticky side of the Decalon down on your print. Start at one corner and work slowly to the other side. Using a squeegie, rub the Decalon firmly from the center out to the edges. Turn over and squeegie on the back.

Now carefully pull the Decalon sheet away, leaving a transparent plastic layer over the print.

Put warm water in a pie tin and soak: Liftable prints, 1 minute; wrapping papers, 15 minutes; cards and wedding invitations, 30 minutes.

Soaking time varies with inks and paper. If the paper won't rub off of the print, just soak longer.

Place your print face down on the hard surface. Peel the paper away from the decal. It is not fragile, so don't be afraid. If using Liftable prints, the paper comes off in one piece. Wipe the back clean with a small sponge. If using other prints, lay it on the hard surface and rub paper off the back with your fingers. Use a sponge to wipe clean.

There is adhesive on the back of your decal. This goes against the plate. Always apply your decal while it is still wet. Make sure the plate is wet also. Put the wet decal in place face up.

With the wet decal in place, press it down against the plate with a wet sponge. Working from the center out to the edges, push out the water and air bubbles. Keep working until it's very smooth. Fold the extra decal around to the back of the plate. When dry, cut away the excess with a razor or scissors.

Rub a little metallic paint on the edge if you like. Your plate can be used for serving or just for display. Don't use a sharp knife on it, though.

Plates like this make such nice gifts. They're as pretty as some decorative plates I've seen in gift shops, too.

· Flower Cart ·

This little flower cart has many possibilities (See Figure 7-9). I made bead flowers to fill it. You may have other ideas.

MATERIALS

nine 8mm yellow beads
twelve 8mm green beads
seven green tri-beads
seven wavy discs: 2 orange, 2
  green, 3 white
orange chenille stem
24″ of ⅞″-wide (#5) orange
  floral ribbon

2″ x 3″ Styrofoam block, 1″ thick
wire frame flower cart
6 plastic greens
42″ of #24 wire
three #16 stem wires
green floral tape
scissors
floral adhesive

INSTRUCTIONS

Cut the #24 wire into 6-inch-long pieces. On one piece, string three green beads. Bend the wire in the middle, bringing the ends together. Keeping the beads at the bend, twist the wire twice snugly against the beads. Push the two wires through the hole in the wavy disc. String one tri-bead onto one of the wires and twist the wire three times to hold the tri-bead, disc and green beads snugly together. Fasten the #24 wires to a piece of stem wire with floral tape.

Make all the flowers in the same manner, using green beads for white and orange discs, and yellow beads for green discs. Cut the stem wires at various lengths.

Fasten the Styrofoam block in the flower cart frame with floral adhesive. Push the stems of the greens into the Styrofoam, one in center back and one on each end. Then fill in with the rest.

Now arrange the flowers in the cart. Use Figure 7-9 as a guide. Make a bow, tie it with chenille stem, shorten the stem, and push into the Styrofoam.

There are so many pretty beads on the market you'll want to try making your own floral designs.

Born and raised in Olney, Illinois, Jane Berry began making hand-crafts as a young girl. Since her marriage in 1951, Jane has been busy raising five children, decorating their home with handcrafted items, and outfitting the family with home sewn fashions.

After her children were all enrolled in school, Jane held her first craft job in a shop in Livonia, Michigan. After relocating to the Media, Pennsylvania, area, she worked for various retail craft outlets and began teaching craft skills and demonstrating new products and methods.

Teaching has brought Jane into contact with scout groups, women's clubs, and evening adult classes. She has contributed short articles to *Creative Crafts Magazine,* is a free-lance designer, and is a member of the Society of Craft Designers.

Jane's varied audiences include educational television viewers, cruise ship classes; and numerous exhibits, bazaars, and trade fairs.